Freedom to Fail

T0087569

Freedom to Fail: Heidegger's Anarchy

Peter Trawny

Translated by Ian Alexander Moore
and Christopher Turner

polity

First published in German as *Irrnisfuge. Heideggers An-archie*, © MSB
Matthes & Seitz Berlin Verlagsgesellschaft mbH, Berlin, Germany, 2014.

The German edition came into being upon the initiative of Sylvie Crossmann
of *Indigène éditions*, the publishing house of Stéphane Hessel's *Time for
Outrage! (Indignez-vous!)*, and appeared concurrently with the
French edition.

Polity Press
65 Bridge Street
Cambridge CB2 1UR, UK

Polity Press
350 Main Street
Malden, MA 02148, USA

ISBN-13: 978-0-7456-9522-8
ISBN-13: 978-0-7456-9523-5 (pb)

A catalogue record for this book is available from the British Library.

Typeset in 12.5 on 15 pt Adobe Garamond
by Toppan Best-set Premedia Limited
Printed and bound in Great Britain by CPI Group (UK) Ltd, Croydon

The publisher has used its best endeavours to ensure that the URLs for
external websites referred to in this book are correct and active at the time of
going to press. However, the publisher has no responsibility for the websites
and can make no guarantee that a site will remain live or that the content is or
will remain appropriate.

Every effort has been made to trace all copyright holders, but if any have been
inadvertently overlooked the publisher will be pleased to include any necessary
credits in any subsequent reprint or edition.

For further information on Polity, visit our website: politybooks.com

Contents

Translators' introduction

There are several noteworthy German terms and their cognates that present difficulties for the English translator, beginning with the original German title of Trawny's book, *Irrnisfuge* or "Errancy-fugue."[1] *Irrnis* is a rare German word that we have always translated as "errancy." As Heidegger employs it, it refers to an originary site of error, rather than to a particular error. When *Irre* is used in this way, as in Heidegger's "On the Essence of Truth," it too is rendered as "errancy." When it is used in a more particular sense, it is rendered as "error." *Irrtum*, for its part, is always rendered as "error." Other related words include *abirren*, *in die Irre gehen*, and *verirren* ("to go astray"), *Abirrung* and *Verirrung* ("aberration"), durchirren ("to wander through"), *irren* ("to err," "to be lead astray"), *Irrfahrt* ("odyssey"), *irrig* and *irrend* ("errant"), and *Irrweg* ("errant path").

The German term *Fuge* can for its part mean both "fugue" (in the musical sense) and "conjuncture." We have translated this term mostly as "conjuncture" or "joint," though occasionally as "fugue," when, for example, Trawny appears to be alluding to Paul Celan's poem "Todesfuge" ("Death Fugue").[2] Other related terms and phrases include *aus den Fugen* ("out of joint"), *Gefüge* ("conjoined structure"), *fügen* ("to join," "to structure"), and *sich fügen* ("to comply").

In several of Heidegger's texts cited by Trawny, Heidegger employs an archaic spelling of the German *Sein* ("to be"), writing it with a "y" rather than with an "i," thus as *Seyn*. Fortunately, an archaic variant of the English word "being" also used to be written with a "y," enabling us (without recourse to neologism) to translate *Seyn* as "beyng." The modern spelling *Sein* has been translated as "being" and its nominalized participle *das Seiende* as "beings."

Ereignis, another Heideggerian *term d'art*, has confounded translators for decades. While, in everyday German, it just means "event," Heidegger often employs it with other valences in mind, such as those of appropriation or bringing something into its own, into what is proper (*eigen*) to it. We have therefore decided to retain both senses by translating it as "appropriative event." Its verbal form (*sich ereignen*), however, has been rendered simply as "to eventuate," although the resonance of appropriation should also be borne in mind.

Finally, unless otherwise indicated, *Anfang* and *anfänglich* have been rendered as "inception" and "inceptual," respectively, since in this text they typically have a deeper sense than the start or beginning of anything whatsoever. *Beginn* has been rendered as "beginning."

When Trawny cites a German translation of a non-German text, we have, except in the case of Imre Kertész's *A gondolatnyi csend, amíg a kivégzőosztag újratölt* ("A Breath-long Silence, While the Fire Squad is Reloading Their Guns"), consulted the original and either provided an existing English translation, or translated the passage from the original ourselves, as with

Jean-Luc Nancy's *La pensée dérobée*. In such cases, reference to the German translation has been omitted. Where Trawny cites a text originally written in German, we have included Trawny's reference to the German edition and provided a reference to an English translation as well, when one exists. Unless otherwise indicated, we have also used the existing English translations in such cases. When no English edition is specified, it means the translation is our own.

Translators' notes and interpolations in the footnotes and the body of the text have been put in square brackets.

We would like to thank Sean Kirkland for encouraging us to take on the translation, as well as Will McNeill for his helpful suggestions concerning a few tricky terms, and especially for his dedication to teaching and translation. Without the countless hours he devoted to helping us improve our German and translation skills, we would not have been able to undertake seriously, let alone complete, this translation.

"Much is monstrous. But nothing / More monstrous than man." Friedrich Hölderlin, translation of the first stasimon of the chorus of Theban elders from Sophocles' *Antigone*.[3]

"*Beyng* itself is 'tragic.'" Martin Heidegger, "Überlegungen XI."

"In this poem, I have sought to bring the monstrousness of the gassings to language." Paul Celan on "Death Fugue."

Freedom to fail: Heidegger's anarchy

The significance of the publication of the *Über-legungen* ["Considerations"], of the so-called *Schwarze Hefte* ["Black Notebooks"], as Heidegger himself referred to them, is still open. Yet they have shown more clearly than everything published previously by him that what he writes in 1961 at the beginning of his *Nietzsche* about the latter – namely, that "the name of the thinker stands as the title for *the matter* of his thinking" – holds also for Heidegger himself: "The matter, the point in question, is itself a confrontation."[4] Heidegger – the name stands for the matter of this thinker, a matter which was always already held to be objectionable, but now with the publication of the *Überlegungen* has become an unavoidable point in question – an unavoidable point in question for anyone who would like to encounter Heidegger's thinking.

Heidegger has no philosophy, no doctrine, that could become the model for an academic school. He once said that himself: "I have no label for my philosophy – and not indeed because I do not have my own philosophy."[5] The assumption that there is a Heideggerian philosophy presupposes that it is a fabricated product, that it can appear as an object, in the form of a book or a collected edition [*Gesamtausgabe*]. Yet he gave the right indication with the motto of his *Gesamtausgabe*: "Paths – not works."[6] The thinker's writings are open attempts. Even the most finished products like *Being and Time* remained incomplete.

This can be seen in his biography as well. When *Being and Time* appeared, Heidegger was 38 years old. Nietzsche reached this age having already worked on the first part of *Zarathustra*. At 38, Schelling's time of publications was already behind him. The thought that in Heidegger's philosophy it was a matter of "paths – not works" is no contrivance, but a fitting self-interpretation. One can learn from Heidegger that philosophy is a philosophizing, always rather a questioning than an answering.

The paths that Heidegger's thinking took are obscure. Ernst Jünger, who was not especially interested in philosophy, once characterized the "forest" as "Heidegger's home": "There he is at home – on untrodden ways, on timber tracks."[7] The paths of thinking led to what is uncertain,[8] into the wild, even into danger. When, in his lecture "On the Essence of Truth" – that turning point in philosophy at the beginning of the 1930s – he explains how "errancy" also belongs to the appropriative event of truth, he hit upon the character of his thinking best of all.

To be "at home" "on untrodden ways" – it is probable that Jünger intentionally brought closely together what is incongruous. Did Heidegger in his thinking want to be at home in the unfamiliar? Assuming this were so: could one explain on the basis of this that it almost irredeemably ended up not only on "timber tracks [*Holzwege*]," but was at times also led astray [*auf Abwege*]? Did not this thinking also move in domains in which there was hardly anything left to think? In which Heidegger in his way ventured to say what need not have been said? Is

3

there a limit to what is to be said, to what *ought* to be said?

The limit, which must be asked about after the publication of the *Überlegungen*, is not that of the unsayable. Heidegger was familiar with this limit. He thought about it with words that are unique in the twentieth century. Yet it is not a matter of this limit. It is a matter rather of the limit that "separates [*scheidet*]" good from evil; "separating into good and evil," which belongs to the "difference [*Unterschied*]" and the "*decision* [Entscheidung]."[9] Should, indeed can, thinking ignore this limit? Should thinking conduct itself with neutrality regarding this limit, acknowledge evil because it belongs to being? Is not Nietzsche the master of all those who have ventured it and continue to do so? Was he Heidegger's master?

Jünger might be right to emphasize the friction between the home and the untrodden in Heidegger's thinking. Here the catastrophe begins, which the thinker recognized in, indeed as, modernity. And was it not especially he, he who occasionally depicted the home so unsentimentally that something threatening also or precisely in its provincial character was revealed

– was it not he who was able to experience the alienations of the twentieth century? It seems obvious that this could be explained dialectically. Yet we have in the meantime come to learn that the whole is more complex. We not only have seen that and how the "planet" stood "in flames" and "the essence of the human" was "out of joint."[10] We also see how thinking is convulsed in its joints and complies with this convulsion.

Thought traverses "the errancy-fugue of the clearing."[11] "Errancy-fugue," a sonorous word, a singular discovery, without allusion.[12] "Errancy," the place or, better, placelessness of error, a landscape of placelessness, an a-topography, which appears as a "fugue" or "conjuncture" [*Fuge*]. The "conjuncture" is for Heidegger what conjoins, what enables a conjoined structure. He thus once spoke of the "errancy-conjoined clearing."[13] "Clearing" is the primary word for truth, for the appropriative event of truth – because truth happens, eventuates. That means, however, that a "conjuncture" of "errancy" – a straying of thinking into that placeless landscape – quite simply builds the "clearing," the eventuating truth, to say it inelegantly. How is that possible?

The formulation "errancy-fugue of the clearing" – we know this from Heidegger – emphasizes the genitive in both senses.[14] It is not that "errancy" brings forth the "clearing" in a one-sided manner. How could the "clearing" emerge from "errancy"? Rather "errancy" stems from the "clearing" as it structures [*fügt*] the latter. The "clearing" is the place in which something like placelessness can first be understood or – only now am I touching on Heidegger – in which placelessness, the loss of place, the significance of place lights up, so that it becomes thinkable that "errancy" belongs to the "clearing."

" 'Errancy-Fugue': Heidegger's An-archy"[15] – I would not have written this essay if I had not thought that here, in this "errancy-fugue," the controversy surrounding the name of Heidegger was gathered, the controversy that is connected *to* the name of Heidegger and the controversy *in* the name of Heidegger that we will have to clarify philosophically. For, if "errancy" structures the "clearing," because the "clearing" needs "errancy," then Heidegger's erring, then his aberrations, are a moment of philosophy.

Here we need to pay attention, as well as to exercise our judgment. For when a philosopher begins to mix what is apparently opposed to truth, i.e., untruth, with truth, to pervert the one into the other, then the sophist is not far away. Is it possible that Heidegger is *the* sophist of modernity? Who would wish to deny that this question is suggested precisely by the publication of the *Schwarze Hefte*? Heidegger unleashes his wrath in them. A thinker appears who hurls his thunderbolts upon everything that cannot withstand the purity of the philosophical gaze. For Heidegger, whoever hearkens to any claim other than those of "thinking and poetry" is lost. In this regard, his rhetoric sometimes cuts capers. Yet ultimately this is not sophistical. The problems do not lie in the ancient quarrel between the philosophers and sophists.

It is solely thinking (and poetry) that provides the world and history with meaning. Only where thinking raises the "*question of the meaning of being*"[16] can it, as the purest form of "Da-sein," weave the strands of meaning belonging to the world and history into a poetic narrative[17] that takes its lead from the drama of tragedy. Not politics, not science, not religion and lastly not even art can claim to have a key role in this narrative – not least because they are incapable of unfolding it. Thinking abandons philosophy and begins – without becoming poetry – to poetize the drama.

What emerges in such a drama is a topography in which the true and the untrue together form the possible, the actual, and the necessary. Yet that still says too little: "Truth, in its essence, is un-truth."[18] The hyphen between "un" and "truth" lets emerge what first of all characterizes the appropriative event of truth in its entirety: where something shows itself as true, "something" conceals itself that – because its significance is not known – leads thought astray. I must note that concealment belongs to this showing. Yet who notices concealment?

Thus the topology of the relation between "errancy" and "clearing" is located in what Heidegger elucidates in a tremendous number of passages as "unconcealment [*Unverborgenheit*]." "Unconcealment" is the more or less literal translation of the Greek word ἀλήθεια. Heidegger consulted the earliest utterances on truth (in Heraclitus, Parmenides, Pindar), understanding later ones (already in Plato) as derivative. That the first path to truth leads to "the" Greeks, is already an aspect of that narrative of tragedy that

Heidegger attempts to transfer to the world and its history.

–

"He who thinks greatly must err greatly,"[19] one reads in Heidegger's collection of sayings entitled "Aus der Erfahrung des Denkens" ["From the Experience of Thinking"]. No doubt it is this experience that Heidegger's philosophy still embodies. Hardly any other thinking in the twentieth century unfolds such an intensity of questioning, even self-questioning, indeed, self-critique. Questioning, thinking, is an experience. Here what counts are not the results of the experience – what counts is the appropriative event of thinking itself. Thinking is a life.

Heidegger would have probably objected that thinking is not a life but a correspondence to being. Certainly. Yet he did live this correspondence; he did grant to thinking unconditional pride of place in everything he did. It was *the* experience – life, it always manifested itself in thinking, found its meaning in it. Only in this way can we understand that this man left behind writings whose possibilities are not fully known even four decades after his death, writings whose truths and errors apparently touch upon the present still more profoundly than the texts of the most contemporary philosophers.

"He who thinks greatly must err greatly" – how often has that saying been commented on scornfully![20] Did Heidegger wish to assert by it that his relation to National Socialism was due to the "greatness" of his thinking? In the text, there is no connection between this saying and Heidegger's relation to National Socialism. Presumably it goes far beyond this connection. Is not *everything* ventured in thinking? Is the venture not the inception of errancy? Yet the reference to the "greatness" of thinking and errancy remains obscure. What does it mean?

In "Überlegungen XIV," a *Schwarzes Heft* from the beginning of the 1940s, Heidegger defines "greatness" ambivalently. It is "the grounding of something inceptual, or, however, since it also has its distorted essence [*Unwesen*],[21] the most extreme hardening of something that has run its course."[22] Every essence has its distorted essence. The essence of greatness lies in the fact that, in history, a decisive caesura, an inception, eventuates. As if this caesura in history had to encounter its refusal, Heidegger recognizes the same greatness in the insensitivity to the inceptual and in the rigidity of an end destined to collapse.

Yet that is by no means its only definition. Indeed, we see how Heidegger repeatedly attempts in the *Schwarze Hefte* to understand greatness as a quality or category of history: "Great is whatever enables freedom to be grounded around oneself and compels one to experience and maintain liberation for freedom as that which is necessary."[23] Of significance here is not only that freedom as such is great, but that the "liberation for freedom," i.e., the "grounding of something inceptual," of an inception of freedom, is as well. Only where an inception eventuates is there freedom.

The greatness of thinking – that formulation need in no way pertain only to Heidegger's own philosophizing. According to its ambivalent meaning, it can show up in an inceptual or a conclusive thinking. In this sense Heraclitus' thinking, as the inception of the history of being, would be just as great as Nietzsche's at the end of metaphysics.

Irrespective, however, of philosophers and their thinking, greatness can doubtless also lie in the appropriative event of the inception itself. For it is only possible for thinking to see the inception when thinking is addressed and called forth by the inception itself. At issue is the fact of an extensive, perhaps traumatic experience. The "liberation for freedom" is no thought. Heidegger is no idealist. It is clear in all that has been said, however, that the ascription of greatness depends on the coordinates of Heideggerian thinking.

As there is a greatness of thinking, there is a greatness of erring. Indeed, Heidegger emphasizes that the philosopher who thinks greatly must necessarily also err greatly. That is certainly an imposing claim. Even if we acknowledge that there is a greatness of thinking, we would not necessarily have to conclude that there is a greatness of erring. Did Kant, for instance, whose thought, we attest, was great, also err greatly? Can the *Critique of Pure Reason* also be characterized as a great error – precisely because it presents a great philosophy? Does Kant err? Perhaps.

In any case, when we consider and unpack the saying further, a kind of uncertainty emerges. What actually is the criterion for determining that a prominent philosophy says something correct, that, in essence, it hits upon the truth? Does this criterion lie in mere success, for example? Yet what does success mean in philosophy? Is there an absolute criterion for the assessment of a philosophy? Where is this criterion? Can it be located anywhere at all other than in the particular philosophy itself? Or is there a place or an appropriative event of truth beyond philosophies? Are we not exposed to a truth that no thinking can ever claim for itself? Only in this way can they be true, and only in this way can they err.

—

When the *Überlegungen II–XV* were published in March 2014, we had to acknowledge that the philosopher not only harbored a private *ressentiment* against Jews, but that he did not shrink from carrying this *ressentiment* over into a philosophical context. The talk of a "world-Jewry," which, "*in an absolutely unlimited way*," assumed "as a world-historical 'task' the deracination of all beings from being,"[24] cannot be understood otherwise than as anti-Semitic.

Reactions were not long in coming. The excitement took on astounding dimensions.

Where one thought that Heidegger's thinking had by and large ceased to have any influence (perhaps because it is without significance in academic German philosophy), it was the public, or its representatives, who now on every continent took up positions and for the most part condemned the philosopher. Not only the statements on 'world-Jewry,' but also the entire content and tone of the *Überlegungen* appeared to prove nothing other than the ultimate bankruptcy of this philosophy.[25]

Not a few readers and interpreters were quickly ready to be very worried. It was above all in Paris that one feared the worst. Which institutions would still be prepared to teach and/or research a possibly anti-Semitic philosophy? The concept of "anti-Semitism in the history of being [*seinsgeschichtlichen Antisemitismus*]"[26] made the rounds, whereby a catastrophic influence on the public perception of Heidegger's thinking was ascribed to it – completely falsely – as if we did not know that every unsuitable concept can be falsified, as if we did not know that public opinion is fickle, and as if we did not know that no secondary literature can ever achieve the power of a philosophy.

The condemnation of Heidegger's thinking outweighed the apologetics. It was clear that it was not grounded in a close reading. Yet it is more than questionable as to whether such a reading will allow the statements on "world-Jewry" to appear in a different light. To judge them anti-Semitic seems to me unavoidable.[27] More harmful than this judgment are attempts to thwart it. Yet what comes of it, and how it might lead us to condemn his entire thought, is another question.

This question has of course already and repeatedly been posed: is not Heidegger's philosophy in general finally finished, now, for example, that his engagement with National Socialism has become known? The question, formulated in this way, demands that questioning cease. One wants to be done with Heidegger, with this thinking that knows no conclusion. Philosophy, however, cannot be brought to a conclusion. What if philosophy did not stop being philosophy even in its errors, in its errancy, indeed in its madness? What if we had to think about philosophy even in the state of its errancy? *What if, even in errancy, we had to – philosophize?* Wouldn't it only then be possible to ask what danger for thinking actually lies hidden in anti-Semitism?

Certainly, we must emphasize that philosophy and anti-Semitism (like every ideological *anti-*) are mutually exclusive. Yet what happens to philosophy when we attempt to exclude it in advance from the danger of anti-Semitism? What happens to philosophy when we separate it from errancy [*Irre*]? Is that even possible? Wouldn't this attempt to immunize philosophy be the worst error [*Irre*]? Overcoming anti-Semitism can only succeed by drawing near to it.

There is an old adage in philosophy that we can only leave a thought or affect behind when we suffer it, go through it. That holds also for anti-Semitism. It is senseless to assume that what would be a task for thought does not hold for the one thinking. Under such an assumption, thinking stops. Yet what is at issue is still something else. Anti-Semitism is tenacious. The opinion that it is always others who are anti-Semites is a cop-out. It is "I" who am the anti-Semite.

–

Since time immemorial, philosophy has presented its image in philosophers. Philosophy

– that was always the philosopher: "I profit from a philosopher only insofar as he can be an example."[28] Nietzsche's oracle is valid, even if modern scientification has introduced the "person of vocation [*Berufsmensch*]" (Max Weber) into philosophy as well. The philosopher, that means Socrates, and together with him Wittgenstein or Heidegger, even if the example that the three set turns out to be entirely different.

Nietzsche asserts that the philosopher sets an example by virtue of his ability to "draw whole nations [*Völker*] after him."[29] "The history of India" in particular proves this. It is important that the example "be supplied by his outward life and not merely in books." It is a matter of "bearing, what they wore and ate, and their morals," and not so much a matter of "what they said, let alone ... what they wrote." The philosopher should be seen, he should leave his writing desk, he should live. And Nietzsche concludes his reflection on a note of resignation: "How completely this courageous visibility of the philosophical life is lacking in Germany!"

Witnesses like Hannah Arendt report that Heidegger was a great teacher. A teacher is truly only a teacher when he sets an example. The image we have of Heidegger includes many features that the philosopher as a university employee does not exhibit: the skier, the cabin dweller, the university rector with the party badge, the philosophical esotericist, the lover, the teacher, the rigorous thinker. It belongs to the image of the philosopher that philosophy conquers and cuts through what is supposedly unphilosophical. About whom can it be said more than about Heidegger that philosophy shapes the philosopher? He represents in every detail a "philosophical life in Germany."

It is not only Heidegger's relation to what is German that determines his philosophical life and shapes it into an image. It is also his understanding, his thinking of the German. "The German alone can originarily poetize and tell of being anew – he alone will conquer the essence of θεωρία anew and finally create *logic*."[30] That sounds as if the philosopher would hand over the philosophical claim to ruling the world to the political claim to do so. Yet even the notion that the task is to "poetize being anew" must be striking. In following out this trace, it quickly becomes clear that Heidegger's conception of the German was at least as wayward in the "Third

Reich" as it is today. Who can believe that the "outcry for the metaphysical poet,"[31] for the "poet of the other inception," for this "most German of Germans,"[32] was heard by anyone other than by Heidegger?

In general, Heidegger must have been sympathetic to much of what Nietzsche wrote in "Schopenhauer as Educator." As when Nietzsche writes, "The only critique of a philosophy that is possible and that proves something, namely trying to see whether one can live in accordance with it, has never been taught at universities."[33] Heidegger would have probably agreed regarding the incapacity and unwillingness of the university. It has no interest in the spirit of philosophy. To be sure, he did not speak of the philosophical life itself. That, however, philosophy presents a unique decision, which concerns everything, is embodied by him on all his paths. Therefore we must emphasize that in this philosophy there is no thought that would have been irrelevant to the philosophical life.

—

Nietzsche's philosopher is Schopenhauer. He profits from him, because Schopenhauer is able to set an example. He sets the example of being "independent of state and society,"[34] thus of *freedom*. Is it an accident that the example of the philosophical life is freedom? No, for the philosophical life is nothing other than the free life, than the life of freedom. To be a philosopher means to be free.

With the question of freedom, the question of morality and ethics is also at stake. Freedom is considered to be the condition of ethics or to be ethics itself. All action, if it is to be ascribed to an agent, is free. Only in this way can we be responsible, become guilty, forgive and ask for forgiveness in order to become guilty again. Free will is the pivot on which all action turns.

Acting and action have an ethical character. Yet not much is said by this. One can assess the action of an individual according to moral criteria, consider it in normative terms as the instantiation of the moral law. One can understand it as the depiction, as the history of a life, in order to acknowledge it as exemplary or reject it as without significance. In the first case we are relating to freedom as the criterion of a moral action, in the second to freedom as a play-space,[35] an open realm, in which this or that is enacted, lived.

The distinction between these two conceptions of freedom is well known: in the first case we are dealing with a positive understanding of freedom, as the freedom *for* … (freedom for good and/or evil); in the second it is a matter of the negative concept as the freedom *from* … (freedom from constraints). I would like to distinguish them according to another criterion: the first freedom is the freedom for a principle, is *principled freedom*; the second is freedom from the principle, is *an-archic freedom*.[36]

Principled freedom organizes our economy of guilt and forgiveness with normative claims. What must I bear? What can I refuse to tolerate? Frequently also: When may I punish, when must I myself be punished? Such questions hinge on the law that is known, that is supposed to come into being before we become familiar with the rights of institutions.

An-archic freedom is an-archy, the inception of a freedom that is nothing besides itself: an "abyss of freedom,"[37] a freedom of the unanticipatable inception. An inception is always an appropriative event, a rupture, an upheaval. It can open up nothing other than the open itself. In it there is no longer any principle to which "Da-sein" or the "subject" could still adhere. In the open there is no obligation [*Verbindlichkeit*] other than to the open itself. This has consequences for thinking and action.

–

Because ethics is an element of philosophy, it is less a question of whether it is an action rather than a way of thinking. Ethics itself is, as a discipline of philosophy, a way of thinking. Indeed, it is much rather a question of whether the sense of ethics is not first fulfilled in action, thus of whether action is not the authentic ethical phenomenon. We would then need to ask further whether someone who is able to do the right thing is not first someone who has learned from thinking what a good deed is.

Kant once self-ironically warned that the "decision," which was "*pure* morality," "by which as a touchstone one must test the moral content of every action," could be rendered "doubtful" "only by philosophers." In "common human reason" it was "long since decided by habitual use, like the difference between the right and the left hand, as it were."[38] Accordingly, the human would, "as it were" by nature, if not shun, at least be able to recognize, the terrible crime as a crime.

The problem of ethics does not lie in the incapacity to recognize the difference between good and evil. Such a being would – according to Kant – no longer come within the scope [*Spielraum*] of reason. Rather, the problem consists in the fact that we are indeed familiar with the difference between good and evil, yet manifestly cannot prevent evil [*Böse*] from happening. We are wicked [*boshaft*], even when we know it. Even if we cannot in our freedom rise above the moral law, this never suffices to determine our action *in conformity with it*. In other words: even when everything in thinking is in the best order, action can lash out into evil. The authentically ethical phenomenon is action.

This is not Heidegger's view. Freedom, the an-archic open, is above all a freedom of thinking. That lies in the relationship between thinking and language: "The hand sprang forth only out of the word and together with the word," one reads in a lecture course from the time when the "planet" stood "in flames." Therefore

Heidegger can indeed say that "The hand acts [*Die Hand handelt*]."[39] Yet that this is so lies in the word, in our relationship to language.

An-archic freedom primarily concerns thinking. Free action springs from the latter. For Heidegger there is no moral law from which human reason could proceed, beyond the appropriative event of truth and the experience of it in thinking. Thinking in an-archic freedom is, then, no longer identical with the ethics of a philosophy that unfolds systematically. That changes nothing about the fact that for Heidegger the human being who refuses the claim [*Anspruch*] of thinking likewise refuses the claim of freedom. Whoever closes himself off from the open in this way not only cannot think, he also cannot act. He follows the models of action of all those technical surrogates of freedom, both subtle and crude. What is convenient in all those patterns of modern life is that no one has to think. Yet that is precisely what we experience [*erleben*] as the greatest freedom.

–

The example that a philosopher sets, if it is to contain Nietzsche's enumeration of "bearing, what they wore and ate, and their morals," is to be illustrated in no other way than in a *narrative*. *The* narrative of the philosophical life is presented in Plato's *Apology*, *Crito*, and *Phaedo*; the philosopher who still remains a philosopher even in mortal danger and in death, whose actions everywhere philosophy itself is. The philosopher is more than the "person of vocation," because philosophy is not a vocation, but rather a life. The excess of life is the freedom that is unfit for vocations. We cannot observe and unfold this excess in any other way than through narrative. This lies in the fact that the example that Socrates sets is precisely the freedom and life of Socrates. The example occurs in the relation between the individual and the universal. The fact of the individual, of the singular, however, can only be narrated.

The concept of narrative includes all non-argumentative speech – and here the meaning of narrative speech is quite extensive. Mythos, poetry, legends and even fairy tales are narratives. That which is singular, individual, stands at the center of narrative. It is possible to narrate the shape of a particular life. However, it is impossible to explain why this shape appears in this way and not another. Heidegger once spoke of a "*mytho-logy of the appropriative event*."[40] Insofar as the "history of being" is a singular history of the singular, it appears as a narrative.

"*Beyng* itself is 'tragic,'"[41] notes Heidegger in the year 1938. He thereby ascribes to "beyng itself" a formal, poetic element. Admittedly, the tragic is put in quotation marks. That is possibly an indication of the fact that Heidegger does not consider the classical text for understanding the tragic, Aristotle's *Poetics*, to be authoritative. Nevertheless, recourse to this text will be helpful in one respect or another. The narrative that Heidegger favors everywhere in his thinking is tragedy.

The narrative, the action, of a life presupposes its freedom. For human life, that is not a relative, but rather an absolute presupposition. Obviously, even the life of a slave can be narrated, for, as a human being, he is free. The life of animals, in contrast, forms no narrative. It is indeed doubtless the case that the animal is "freer" than a machine, which is not even not free. Yet neither in the principled nor in the an-archic sense can an animal actually be free. The essence of the animal is never out of joint.

Even the human being of tragedy is free, for he acts within the open. The plot[42] of tragedy does not present a moral, yet it does present an ethics – an "originary ethics" even.[43] That is what Heidegger emphasizes in his way in the "Letter on 'Humanism.'" What ἦθος means would be shown not so much by "Aristotle's lectures on 'ethics'" as by the "tragedies of Sophocles."[44] What they "say" is in this respect "more inceptual"; certainly also – though not only – because tragedy does not speak about ethics, but is ethics in word and deed.

–

For Heidegger, freedom is the "letting-be of beings,"[45] which goes out beyond beings. A free action and thought is a "letting oneself engage" "with the open and its openness in which every being comes to a stand." The open, however, is precisely truth itself, "unconcealment," ἀλήθεια. The narrative of the history of being is contained in this thought and with it the story of Heidegger's thinking and life.

Unconcealment is not mere openness or pure light. The metaphorics of light, of which Heidegger here and there avails himself, in any case does not capture the sense of unconcealment. Heidegger proceeds from the fact that things which show themselves need an "open place" in order to appear. Yet this open place itself springs from a prior concealment and remains bound up with it. Unconcealment is "un-*concealment*," a concealment that recedes in favor of something opened up, as it is "*un*-concealment," the openness that recedes in favor of something previously concealed. In the metaphorics of light, light is always the source of the shadow, yet openness is not simply the source of concealment. Openness and concealment reciprocally refer to one another.

This unsublatable interplay of concealment and openness is the "truth of being." It forms the topography in which human freedom is actualized. A consequence of this is that action is not only related to things that show themselves. At first glance, this relation presents itself as unproblematic. What shows itself can be procured and worked on. In the world of production everything is present and available – together with apparatuses that make visible what is not present and available per se. Everything that can be objectified can become the object or standing-reserve of technicity and the economy. Everything pertaining to technicity and economics can be planned and organized. For Heidegger even science belongs to such planning, since it is necessarily related to objects.

Yet beyond these appearing objects, action is also related to concealment itself. The human being forgets this relation, he must forget it, since he is constantly occupied with what appears. For Heidegger, to forget the relation to concealment means "*erring*."[46] Yet concealment must necessarily be forgotten. Attention to concealment is hardly imaginable. Erring is therefore not a mistake of thinking or action. For the philosopher, errancy is rather the "open site for and ground of *error*." In this passage, Heidegger's feeling for language becomes evident. For "error" is "the kingdom (the dominion) of the history of those entanglements in which all kinds of erring get interwoven." What predominates in history is error and errancy. All so-called facts are only the surface of a depth of meaning that withdraws. The narrative begins.

There are various kinds of erring in which thinking and acting become entangled. Heidegger cites the "most ordinary wasting of time, making a mistake, and miscalculating," "going astray" and "venturing too far in one's essential attitudes and decisions." The one thinking and acting errs whenever he forgets concealment and what is concealed. A relation to this concealment can therefore take place only in thinking. Concealment announces itself – if at all – in recognition [*Erkenntnis*].[47] For Heidegger, the ethical precedence of thinking is grounded in this. Only he who thinks can actually act.

Errancy, the "open site for error," is "the essential counteressence to the inceptual essence of truth,"[48] to "unconcealment," to ἀλήθεια. Errancy belongs to thinking. It is a counteressence [*ein Gegenwesen*], a counter- [*ein Gegen*], a region [*eine Gegend*], that belongs to the essence itself and is not the nonessence that Heidegger considers to be a "deformation."[49] The appropriative event of truth is not contingently, but necessarily likewise the appropriative event of errancy. Heidegger meant precisely this when he said: "He who thinks greatly must err greatly."

The appropriative event of truth, the interplay of openness and concealment, is errancy. If that is possible, then Heidegger himself can still err when he speaks of errancy: the thought of errancy is then itself errant. Suddenly it appears that the truth claim which Heidegger's thinking makes has a very unusual character. Does it perhaps only want to tell us about itself – and thereby itself still leave entirely open what is true and what is false?

–

This has consequences for "knowledge [*Wissen*]." Not only do the *Überlegungen*, the *Schwarze Hefte* from 1931 to 1941, demonstrate unmistakably that the philosopher rejects the knowledge proper to science. Knowledge, which complies with the modern demand for "certainty" (*certitudo* in Descartes), projecting itself as *mathesis universalis*, as a universal cognition [*Erkenntnis*] going back to mathematics, has nothing to do with philosophical thinking. Its propensity for control and organization is completely and utterly of a technical nature.

Heidegger, in contrast, has an "*authentic* knowledge" in view.[50] Knowledge is the "preservation of the truth of beyng." That is not simply a knowledge of. ... The truth of being is no object. Yet one cannot know a non-object.

Knowledge as preservation is therefore a type of enactment [*Vollzug*], a type of action. Thus Heidegger can also say that this knowledge "stands *in* the truth."[51] Knowledge – a moment of the appropriative event of truth. Only insofar as truth eventuates is knowledge possible.

The one who knows is thus in no way someone who has at his disposal a specific kind of knowledge [*Wissen*], someone who is a scientist [*Wissenschaftler*]. The one who knows is, according to Heidegger, a "Da-sein" that finds himself in a relation to the appropriative event of truth and preserves this relation. We do not have knowledge; we are knowledge. Yet to the extent that errancy belongs to the appropriative event of truth, knowledge, precisely because it is standing-in-the-truth, is always also an erring.[52]

That attests to the "finitude of philosophy."[53] Belonging to the appropriative event of truth has a spatiotemporal character, according to which thinking is not capable of surveying the totality of meanings. All knowledge that even merely strives for such an overview misunderstands its belonging to the appropriative event of truth. By claiming to know [*erkennen*] the structure of its elements, it wants, as it were, to freeze the appropriative event. It knows nothing of the errancy that occurs in and together with truth. Yet although it knows nothing of it, it nevertheless still belongs to it.

There is no institution, perhaps no place, for such knowledge. It is a knowledge that can only unfold as a thinking (or poetry) of being, can only become an unfolding of the history of being. Yet it will never lead to the clear and distinct knowledge that the scientist claims for himself. Nor will it facilitate an argumentative and critical discourse. Being-in-the-truth is not a question of argument, but rather of co-thinking and co-acting. Contentious discourse must avail itself of objective ascriptions in order to be able to be discourse. To be in the truth means to renounce such ascriptions.

In practice, however, philosophical thinking cannot renounce objective knowledge. Philosophizing presupposes an acquaintance with philosophy. If this acquaintance is itself philosophical (and not merely an acquaintance *with* philosophy), it is no more, yet no less, than the presupposition of existing in the philosophical life of the errancy of truth – in its appropriative event. The difference consists in whether philosophy maintains a purely historiographic attitude to an archive or whether this archive becomes the point of departure for a philosophical way of thinking and life. This touches upon the crisis of contemporary philosophy.

—

The ordinary understanding of truth is based on the statement or the proposition or the speech act, in each case on a meaning represented by a rational subject. The statement can be held to be true or false insofar as its correspondence or non-correspondence with its object can be ascertained. Or it is presumed to be free of contradictions. Or a speech act asserts a justified or unjustified validity claim. Deciding what is true always takes place in the logical realm, in language and in speech.

The possibility of distinguishing true and false is rational; it is ascribed to reason and to the rational subject. In this sense, only a human being (or God) can distinguish true statements from false ones. The ζῷον λόγον ἔχον, the living being that has language, is the living being that knows the difference between truth and falsity. All the aforementioned conceptions of truth go back to this definition of the human, which can be found in Aristotle.

This leads to the opinion that predominates today, namely, that philosophies are in competition for the "better argument."[54] Beyond "argumentation" there is no "explicitly rational behavior." That is supposed to be the fundamental feature that distinguishes philosophy, according to Habermas. It is thereby presupposed that every rational subject can gauge what a better argument in general is. That turns out to be a difficult matter in relation to the logical presuppositions for the optimizability of meanings. In any case it holds that the subject's reason is the pivotal element of arguments. They are organized around the distinction between true and false. The argument relates to an object, it itself has objective meaning. In a world of objects it is effective.

The respective theories of truth (from the correspondence theory to the semantic theory of truth to the theory of argument, etc.) are logics. Yet because they correspond to the reason of the subject, it can come to appear that truth is the aspect of a subjective competency. Then truth is drawn into the act of being right and of justification. From there the subject, in being right, raises the claim to also being privileged on the basis of the correctness of its statements. Indeed, the assertion of its own claims becomes the primary motivation for speech. Sophistry and the argument grow from the same stem.

Being right, which invokes a justification that is internal to the various claims, is often enough an element of philosophical discussions in which the matter discussed melds with the opinions that the subject is advocating. It may be that even the matter discussed profits from the dynamic of the argumentation. In the end, however, the facticity of the argumentative vanity produces such a one-sided effect that nothing appears any more other than the subject, which, in light of the truth that has been gained, puts everything else in the shadows. That the subject is right is, then, identical with the place in the sun for which it is always striving.

Heidegger's conception of truth has nothing to do with all that. For him, the criterion is not the logical organization of statements, speech acts, or arguments, but rather the truth of being, the appropriative event of the interplay of openness and concealment. This happens outside of statements, speech acts, and arguments. It is therefore not something that can be organized or controlled or immobilized by the subject. It manifests itself as a singular disempowerment of the subject. That Heidegger's thinking frequently meets a brusque rejection perhaps has to do with this disempowerment.

—

Heidegger, by the way, does not assert that stating, speaking, and arguing are not connected with the truth of being. The freedom of the human being consists in letting himself engage in the open and the concealment belonging to it. He does this by speaking. To this extent, the statement, the speech act and the argument, the reason of the subject, stand in a special relation to truth. What is problematic in this outlook, however, is that truth as such is reduced to its logical organization. The truth is overwhelming, greater than speech.

For Heidegger, the human being is not the subject that organizes its truth. Rather, he experiences the fact that truth eventuates as his "*exposure*."[55] Exposure – this means insecurity, being

37

at the mercy of, a dearth of protection. Exposed to the sun, to violence. The exposure of Dasein – Dasein as exposure – is an experience of freedom. Foundering, the collapse of hope, is an action unknown to the animal. Suicide, only possible for the human being, is an echo of freedom, as is the propensity for habit, for routine.

Exposure is an-archic freedom, exposure to an-archia itself. In it the routine of history collapses with dreadful regularity. The drama of upheavals and revolutions, of crimes and wars, arises without warning. Life, only just secure on its path, suddenly stands in flames. That holds not only for *the* grand narrative of history, but even for the histories of individuals who, in the era of total normalization, meld ever less frequently with the great narrative.

In this exposure the logical organization of truth shatters. It comes to experience its impotence and begins to appropriate these processes as irrational. Yet the dissociation of the irrational points to the weakness of such thinking. The exposure is an overflow of meaning that is supposed to be halted by the difference between the rational and irrational. The excess is supposed to cease. The freedom is too free. Habit belongs to habitation.

In all the decisions on which we rely, in all the criteria according to which we act, freedom is forgotten. In all the true and false statements by which we direct ourselves, truth is forgotten. Yet forgotten is not synonymous with: not there. Truth and freedom eventuate, even if we forget them. That is errancy.

—

The truth of being is onto-tragic. This is connected with the first of all inceptions, the inception of the history of being. It begins with the appropriative event of ἀλήθεια, the reciprocal happening of opening up and concealment. A narrative element thereby flows into the history of being. Aristotle speaks in his *Poetics* of μῦθος. The plot is the origin and soul of tragedy.[56] Thinking and acting are figures of an-archic freedom. Considered from the perspective of the inception, everything is open. Yet, within being, there is opened up at the same time a form of occurrence, a plot, in which the openness of being takes shape.

Mythos, the plot of the tragedy, turns on transgression, foundering. This is attested to in the commonplace proverb, "to err is human." This proverb has a long tradition. It surfaces in Christian and Stoic contexts. Yet it stems from tragedy or its milieu. Sophocles and Euripides are familiar with it. Theognis uses it, a poet who lived in the second half of the 6th century BC, cited by Plato in the *Laws*. In Sophocles it appears in *Antigone*.[57] Tiresias exhorts Creon: "Think upon this, my son! All men are liable to make mistakes." However, the seer makes clear that even in errancy one can still think things over, that one can still change one's mind. Yet Creon is concerned with something else. He does not hear the warning and founders.

Decisive for the possibility of erring, according to Heidegger, is the form of occurrence of being itself: unconcealment. With reference to *Antigone*, he once explained that "the human being" is "placed into the site of his historical abode, into the πόλις, because he and he alone comports himself toward beings as beings, toward beings in their unconcealment and concealing, and can be mistaken within the being of beings, and at times, that is, continually within the most extreme realms of this site, must be mistaken within being, so that he takes nonbeings to be beings and beings to be nonbeings."[58] The plot of being is a choreography of erring dictated by unconcealment. The cities totter, the state before collapse …

Our thinking and acting, especially, though not only, in the political community, is exposed to an-archic freedom – "originary errancy."[59] We are not in the position to see through all the presuppositions and consequences of our thinking and acting. Concealment always occurs together with openness. It makes every certainty illusionary. Because we do not dominate this appropriative event, we must go astray; foundering is inevitable. Tragedy gives to this an-archic freedom its inceptual shape. The thinker – Heidegger – exposes himself to its tragic choreography.

–

The "name" of "finitude" is "most often poorly understood. It is understood as a lack that one deplores and that one hopes to be remedied. Yet this word must be understood in a completely different way."[60] And Nancy adds in a footnote: "This other understanding is the only real thing to accomplish on the basis of Heidegger's oeuvre." Nancy is right. The understanding of finitude is a key to Heidegger's thinking.

The range of understanding encompasses the finitude of Dasein and that of beyng, in other words, the finitude of the "turn" – of this revolution – in beyng. The finitude of Dasein and of beyng is not a lack, because it is characteristic for both the one and the other. Dasein, affected by death, is a "*being toward the end*."[61] Because history belongs to beyng, "finitude and uniqueness"[62] characterize it.

This has immeasurable consequences. One of them consists in Heidegger not granting any supra-temporality to the questions and concepts of philosophy – a refusal of Platonism and metaphysics, for which the ideas are eternal. What a strange challenge to thinking Heidegger entertains here: with the rejection of Platonism, the distinction that is presupposed in classical philosophizing between the universal and the particular falls away. Everything becomes singular and finite – even truth. This leads to the fact that, as far back as antiquity, various modes of truths must be differentiated. The appropriative event of truth is logicized already early on. At the end of this history, the only thing left is correctness and being right.

This in turn leads to the fact that philosophizing in each case becomes finite. Kant was able to think the categorical imperative only precisely within the historical moment in which he thought it. The categorical imperative in Heraclitus? Impossible. Heidegger himself makes use of the same thing. The question concerning the meaning of being, the truth of being, could only be found in a topography in which modernity threatens to abolish being in general. Heidegger's thinking is Heidegger's history.

Finitude, however – and this is important – is conceived as a formal element of Dasein and beyng. The example Heidegger employs both in *Being and Time* and in the *Contributions to Philosophy* is that of "ripeness."[63] Ripeness is completion. The ripe fruit is the completed fruit. The individual Dasein, like the history of being, is poetically rhythmized. Rhythm is oriented towards completion. Its catastrophic fruit is the completion of metaphysics in the slaughters and extermination camps of the Second World War. Heidegger's thinking nearly perished from it.

Because Heidegger's thinking delivers itself over to and follows this poetic rhythm, it knows an archeology as well as an eschatology. History and, in history, the individual Dasein are formed constructs. They have a beginning [*Anfang*], a middle, and an end.[64] Mythos, the plot of tragedy, demands tribute. It determines the rhythm of thinking and acting within the rhythm of history.

Thinking and acting move within a history that, for Heidegger, is to be understood only in terms of drama. Heidegger's philosophy resides in the narrative of an inception, whose possibilities are fulfilled in ends that are to be narrated differently in each case. Thinking and action are subsumed under this narrative. I think and act always in a world, in a place, at a particular time, upon an earth.

—

Reality is narrated. If Heidegger wishes to come to learn [*erfahren*] something about Russia, he does not read a statistical survey on the difference between city and country; rather, he reads Dostoyevsky. The same is of course true for Germany. Hölderlin poetizes what it means to be German. In the history of being, even philosophy becomes the plot of a Western narrative. Empirical research, the discipline of history, ignores or ruins the narrative. For this reason, Heidegger despises it. Hardly any concept in the history of being makes the narrative, and hence unhistoriographic, character of this history as clear as the concept of "decline" does.

Already in the Summer Semester of 1920, Heidegger occupied himself with Oswald Spengler's *The Decline of the West*; certainly very critically, yet he evidently read the book with interest immediately after its appearance (the first volume appeared in 1918; the second followed in 1922). He keenly took note of Spengler's project. In 1941, in "Überlegungen XV," he refers once again to the book. "Europe," one reads, is the "actualization of the *Decline of the West*." Thus there exists "not the slightest occasion to declaim against the 'author' Oswald Spengler."[65]

Heidegger thought the decline differently than Spengler, though. What he has to say about it belongs in the narrative of a tragic beyng.

It is not a mere end, but rather the caesura that links the end and the inception. "Decline, in the singular, elevated sense of the history of beyng, is the re-turn into the sheltering [*Bergung*] of the not-yet-unconcealed [*Noch-Unentborgenen*]." "In this way, the decline becomes the authentic and inviolable preservation of the truth of beyng [*Wahrung der Wahrheit des Seyns*]." In other words, in the history of beyng, the decline [*Untergang*] is "never an end," but rather "a beginning." Yet it can "only" be this "where emergence [*Aufgehen*], having sprung forth in terms of the appropriative event, reaches into the favor of the true-ness [*Wahrheit*] of beyng."[66]

The decline thus happens when those who "truly decline" experience the "more inceptual emergence" in the "abyss" of the "true-ness of beyng," in the deepest concealment as "sheltering of the not-yet-unconcealed." Yet who are those who "truly decline"? They are those who recognize in the choreography of tragic beyng that the decline must happen. Those who decline comply, they hearken to the poetic rhythm of being, they are – in the eyes of the thinker – ripe for sacrifice.

The decline is no thought. It has a lethal reference in the happenings of the time. It is no wonder that Heidegger first began to ponder it in the final years of the war. The decline of the "contemporary human being" was supposed to be connected with the decline of the belligerent nations of the Second World War – not to say: to the decline of the Germans – consummation in the catastrophe towards the first emergence from the ashes.[67] Since neither the one nor the other figure of history thought about wanting to decline, Heidegger came to the conclusion that even the decline still had to remain "refused." Yet it remained refused because "historylessness" had begun.

–

Heidegger expected the decline; indeed, this was a necessary happening in the rhythm of the history of being; in other words, it would have been a necessary happening if it had happened. The "final act" of the "*highest completion of technicity*"[68] would be achieved when "the earth itself blows up" and "current humanity" disappears. That would be no "misfortune" but rather the "first purification *of being* from its deepest deformation by the supremacy of beings." A deluge must come to wash away the dreck of technicity.

Such evocations are not worth speaking of in philosophical terms. They obtain a sense only in the narrative of being. In it, the Second World War, with all its monstrous phenomenal metastases up to and including the Shoa and Hiroshima, stood for a world-historical eruption from which the world was supposed to emerge transformed. In such an expectation it is in any case evident that these times offered a *non plus ultra* to extermination and transgression. If nothing were to change now, then when would it?

Heidegger's thought betrays what the philosopher was: the final and probably most vehement obstructer of modernity. The *Schwarze Hefte* are nothing other than the wild attempt to combat the project of the "disenchantment of the world" by any philosophical and non-philosophical means available. And the Second World War more and more turned out to actually be a line of demarcation behind which everything that Heidegger loved, that in which and from which he lived, disappeared irretrievably.

What disappeared is a world that even today still tenaciously defends its survival. Homeland, border, earth, poetry, place, community, ambiance, all of that can no longer raise any claims within technicity's universal transit space. And if a voice makes itself heard, seeking to defend what was self-evident in former times, then that happens and must happen within the universal transit space of the medium itself.[69] Even Heidegger presented the text "Why Do we Stay in the Provinces?" on a Berlin radio broadcast – and unintentionally did so *ad absurdum*.

Technicity produced a universal topography in which the human being circulates with breathless excitement. In principle tuned to a fever pitch and by no means burned out, he integrates himself into this topography without knowing of any idea that could proscribe his integration. There are certainly islands of intimacy,[70] yet these have to affirm their worldlessness. What was lost can thus preserve itself.

The post-war era today presents itself as a successive normalization of relations. The military conflicts were outsourced and at least ideologically outlawed. Economic conditions in the affluent states have become so stabilized that rebellions, let alone revolutions, appear less real than "[u]nicorns and fairy queens."[71] The virtual world of the medium channels every passionate yearning into intellectual and physical masturbation. The relations of life have congealed into a leaden uneventfulness.

It is possible that Heidegger understood himself as someone who could put a stop to such conditions. Yet that line of demarcation runs its course in his own thinking. It turns desperately against modernity, to which it essentially belongs. The berserk eruptions in the *Schwarze Hefte* are no different.

—

In questions of ethics, the "saying" of the "tragedies of Sophocles" is "more inceptual" than the "*Nicomachean Ethics*" of Aristotle. Tragedy contains an ethics of ἀλήθεια, an ethics of an-archic freedom. That is "originary ethics." Because the plot of ἀλήθεια is tragedy, the ethics of the appropriative event of truth, the ethics of the origin, is a tragic ethics.

In the truth of being, errancy is not only inevitable; it belongs as an essential possibility to truth itself. At issue is not that we err once in a while, but that errancy is at the center of the whole, the heart of tragedy. If Oedipus did not err, the plot, his action, would not be tragic. An ethics of unconcealment in the sense of a tragic ethics is an ethics of errancy.

Yet the ethical significance of erring is not apparent – at least when we consider the tragedies of Sophocles. Nothing universal can be derived from the foundering of Oedipus, not even a normative morality. It is precisely this, however, that Heidegger could have understood to be the advantage of tragedy and its ethics. Errancy, in any case, offers no possibility to ascribe to Oedipus guilt or responsibility – core concepts of a normative morality.

The human being of history is – Oedipus. He errs tragically, guiltlessly, without responsibility [*verantwortungslos*]. At one point in the "Country Path Conversation," Heidegger speaks of an "enigmatic region, where there is nothing for which we can answer [*verantworten*]." This is so, "Because it is the region of the word that alone answers for itself." "For us it remains only to hear the answer befitting the word."[72] A moral responsibility is rejected in favor of a responsibility in the sense of a correspondence to the word. Seen in this way, errancy would be a mishearing [*Verhören*] from which a discordant answer to the word would necessarily arise.

This mishearing, disaccord [*Ungemäßheit*], or lack of measure [*Unmäßigkeit*] – indeed what is excessive [*das Übermäßige*] – belongs to the appropriative event of truth, characterizing it outright. It is a moment of an-archic freedom, in which erring can in no way be interpreted in terms of guilt. An-archic freedom is a freedom from responsibility and guilt. Just as Oedipus cannot be guilty of having slept with his mother, the one who errs is not guilty of having foundered in the interplay of concealment and openness. In the appropriative event of truth, moral responsibility is merely a phantasm.

The morality of revenge and forgiveness is just as phantasmatic. Heidegger is in this respect a student of *Zarathustra*: "For *that mankind be redeemed from revenge*: that to me is the bridge to the highest hope and a rainbow after long thunderstorms."[73] Revenge – that is the impossibility of freedom, the perpetuation of bad action, genuine evil [*Übel*]. To be sure, tragedy is familiar with a redress in catastrophe, yet not with revenge. It emphasizes recognition, self-recognition, in the moment of errancy. It reveals that revenge is senseless. One cannot avenge oneself on someone who errs; he is guiltless, and one cannot forgive him.

Could that be the inception of a tragic ethics, of an ethics without revenge or guilt, an ethics of abyssal freedom?[74] Heidegger is indeed right that the ethics of tragedy is not one of revenge, guilt, and conscience, yet there is nevertheless a redress, a suffering, that corresponds to the excess of errancy. After Oedipus has seen through the fact that he acted in errancy, after, in the communications of that messenger from Corinth,[75] peripeteia has eventuated, he gouges out his eyes – as if his eyes, which finally saw and recognized such erring, their own blindness, had to be blinded forever in order to retain their sight. Without this redress that belongs to errancy, tragedy would not be tragic. Yet this compensatory suffering is not made thematic in Heidegger's understanding of errancy, and thus it is not made thematic in his understanding of " 'tragic' beyng."

The thought of errancy – if it is to be interpreted ethically – thereby runs the risk of portraying a senseless construct. If erring leaves behind no trace in the one who errs, then the sense of what can be designated as errancy becomes untenable. Admittedly, the fact that it is not experienced as such may belong to errancy in the happening of truth. Yet in what respect, then, can it still be distinguished from hitting upon the true? Does not the whole talk of errancy become a farce if it does not affect the one erring? Must not the one erring suddenly realize that he erred? Yet what does it mean to err?

–

Peripeteia is the announcement of catastrophe. Oedipus and Creon and Hippolytus – they all recognize that they erred. It is a recognition that leads to catastrophe. In tragedy, this recognition cannot have any moral significance. Yet recognition is introduced by peripeteia. In Heidegger's understanding of errancy, both recognition and peripeteia seem to be missing. Ultimately, truth and errancy appear to be the same.[76]

The criterion for distinguishing truth and errancy is missing. For Heidegger, it is precisely a matter of understanding and thinking this lack. Whoever errs cannot separate the aberration from the true. This is not a problem of awareness. It is false to suppose that the awareness of errancy has anything to do with errancy. No one acts with so much unawareness that he does not know what he does. Yet reflection never reaches the truth. The awareness of errancy remains excluded from this. It is all the same what I suppose or intend. I err.

In spite of this, there must be moments in which the engulfment of the happening of truth opens up, when clearer insight into the true and errant paths of thinking emerges. Yet how to retain this insight? Thinking and acting keep moving. Insight is carried away by action. Thinking can only be tragic because it does not surpass the plot of history. It remains immanent to the propulsion of finitude. Even peripeteia cannot completely end errancy. The true end of tragedy can only be the possibility of errancy. That holds for the tragedy of Oedipus as for the tragedy of being.

What is terrifying about Heidegger's understanding of truth, what is terrible about an-archic freedom, is that he holds the criterion that can distinguish the true from the false to be the result of a thinking that has given up the "abyss of freedom." The kind of thinking that begins to follow a clear and distinct criterion of truth has robbed itself of its freedom. It has aligned itself with the certainty of the rational. It has committed itself to technicity, in order to make the tragedy of being impossible.

Assuming for a moment that Heidegger, with the entire resoluteness of his thinking, had given up the orientation to a logical criterion of truth in favor of belonging to the appropriative event of truth and errancy, then what thought would have been able to appear to him in advance as false and unthinkable? Thinking must err ...

–

The catastrophe, however, is not a single negative occurrence, not an accident. It belongs to Heidegger's strengths to discover and present the most exciting possibilities of thought. It is the human being who is "in his essence himself a καταστροφή."[77] He is a "reversal that turns him away from his own essence." "Among beings," he is "the sole catastrophe."

The human being, the sole catastrophe. For, nothing else can turn away from its own essence, can fall away from its own essence. The decline, the fall, is only possible for him. At the same time, that means that the human being is the only being [*Wesen*] that has its own or proper essence at all.

For Heidegger that is in fact the case. This condition, this being [*Sein*], which is located in its proper essence, can be grasped in different ways. There was a phase in Heidegger's thinking in which he wanted to connect this authentic essence with the community of the people [*Volk*]. He called upon the Germans to let the truth of history be handed over to them by the Greeks. Sophocles' tragedy had found its echo in Hölderlin's Hymns, in his *Empedocles*. Those who acted tragically were the solitary ones who foundered on their countrymen.

Heidegger wanted to narrate this history to the Germans. He wanted to determine a role for them to play in it. Presumably he occasionally saw in himself just such an Empedocles, who, cast out by his own people, threw himself into Etna. Thinking foundered. Here different histories are overlaid. They must be unraveled more precisely.

The markedly tragic determination of the human being's essence is that he cannot hold on to the state of remaining within his own essence. He continually deviates from himself, falls away from himself, founders. This foundering is for Heidegger not a bad thing. To be outside oneself, the ecstasy of the flame and the fall, belongs to freedom. The human being falls because he aims too high – that is the tragic essence of the human being, the catastrophe.

If the human being should ever be this catastrophe then he will have attained his essence. The narrative imperative runs: Be Oedipus! Be tragic! Yet it came about altogether differently.

–

The difference between good and evil is a distinction in being. "In the clearing," there is "healing." Yet with the latter, "evil" also appears. The "essence" of evil consists, however, "not in the mere baseness of human action," but rather "in the malice of rage." And Heidegger decisively adds to this: "Both of these, however, healing and the raging, can essentially occur in being only insofar as being itself is in strife."[78] Because the appropriative event of truth is errancy, good and evil can happen. Indeed, good and evil are regions of a historical topography in which the human being is errantly underway.

Raging goes beyond the baseness of human action. Raging is a tension that is ready to snap. It happens – essentially, in such a way that the human being would not be able to assume responsibility. That there is raging is an appropriative event that needs the human being in order to attain actuality. Clearly, thinking and acting are threatened by rage, letting themselves be afflicted by it. Yet no individual deed ever reaches the evil of the "malice of rage" itself.

This holds for *every* deed, i.e., even for the most un-imaginably bad. Doing and acting move always already between things of the world. They are already entangled in everyday affairs. They never reach the "strife" of being itself; nor can they think the appropriative event of truth. The problem of evil can therefore not be decided in action. Only thinking can set off on the path of understanding evil.

In order to become familiar with errancy, it must be thought. It is by thinking that we gain access to the appropriative event of truth, to understanding it. For this reason, the problem of evil is not one of morality – at any rate not a morality that is decided only in action. Morality has no inkling of the appropriative event of truth, but rather holds itself to laws and rules that spring from reason, not being.

Therefore it is also a misunderstanding to maintain that the human being could be morally responsible for evil. Such a thought shirks the question of genuine evil. The latter never lies in historiographic occurrences, but rather in an origin of these occurrences. This origin is concealed in the appropriative event of errancy. What is first of all terrible according to Heidegger is not that we kill, but that we do not heed whence the freedom of killing stems. It is absurd to believe that Heidegger would have welcomed the killing that has been present throughout history. But if history is errancy, then pain belongs to it.

At one point, Heidegger remarks: "The evil and therefore most acute danger is thinking itself, insofar as it has to think against itself, yet can seldom do so."[79] We recall that Hannah Arendt characterized the "banality of evil" as "thoughtlessness."[80] For Heidegger evil belongs to thinking. Insofar as it elucidates being, it elucidates evil. For even evil belongs to the world-narrative. A world beyond evil – a world beyond history.

–

Who bears the guilt of history? Who holds the lever of the "monstrous"? Is Hitler responsible? Did he set the planet on fire? Or Mao? Does Eichmann bear the responsibility for Auschwitz? Or is it a group of large-scale criminals, a clique behind the scenes, that is guilty? Who bears the guilt for Birkenau? The Wannsee Conference? Is the German guilty? Is Heidegger guilty? Do we need culprits? Are we put at ease when we know who the culprits are?

The victims lend gravity to these questions. They are what hinders them, what makes them appear perhaps inhuman. The victims are the trace of a guilt that needs culprits. The victims are the trace of a history that challenges us to identify the culprits. Yet where does this trace end? Does it ever end?

A history without culprits – is unbearable.

—

Heidegger would not be the thinker he is if he had not narrated the tragic history all the way to the end. For him, not only it is unquestionable that his thinking is subsumed entirely under this. In order to be able to be thinking at all, participation in this grand narrative is necessary. Thinking is not only in history; it is itself history.

For "essential thinking," the "freedom for error, long, useless erring, from which only those who are determined and attuned to thinking 'learn' what is essential to them,"[81] is a sort of self-confirmation. The "history of philosophy is to be sure not the 'history' of errors in the sense of the historiographic apposition of one inaccuracy after the other." Rather, it is "in itself an odyssey in which errancy has come to be experienced [*eine Irrfahrt, in der die Irre erfahren ... werde*], and every time a cleft in the truth of beyng is intimated." Here "we are by no means experienced enough travelers [*fahrtentüchtig*] to wander through [*durchirren*] this history, without ending up in the ascertainment of the false, or, what is of the same value, in empty commendations of philosophers." The "decided non-scientific status of philosophy" can only be ventured when the philosophers are resolved "to wander through the errant paths of their history – i.e., to think these paths only as those who question from the ground up."

The position from which the *Schwarze Hefte* were written is of this sort. The an-archic freedom of thinking demands, as an-archic questioning, a "freedom for error." To venture this freedom liberates one from science and liberates one for history. An-archic thinking goes on an odyssey [*Irrfahrt*]. The alternative – the technical procedure [*Verfahren*] of science – is its untragic end. Being without error is technical routine. Thinking ceases.

Heidegger's thinking branched off into paths, claiming to try to find its way on them. Indeed, this thinking is one that attempts not an experimenting thinking in the narrow, i.e., natural-scientific sense, but rather one that strides into uncertain, into the most uncertain, realms. On these paths, the an-archic freedom of thinking unfolds in its own way; indeed, it is dramatically orchestrated. The drama of thinking – hardly any philosophy has performed it like Heidegger's.

He was aware of this more than others were. He knew what his thinking, his erring, demanded of him. The "one erring" must "also bear the fact that what is false and missing and ambiguous and polysemous" about him, insofar as he still advocates it, will be "reckoned to be what he actually 'intended,' and thus the entirety of his thinking will then be discarded."[82] One of the dangers of erring consists in our not recognizing wherein we err. How, then, is the other supposed to be able to? Yet we probably notice it earlier, but then cannot prevent the other from taking the error for what was "actually intended." Thus does errancy inevitably introduce an asymmetry in understanding. What the thinker recognized as errancy his reader accepts as what is true.

In this respect, Heidegger's elucidations of the finitude of thinking are convincing. He never succumbed to the temptations of the absolute in Hegel's sense; he also rejected science's claim to a progressive knowledge. He took the orientation towards poetry – of course Hölderlin's poetry above all – so far that only the fewest have followed and will follow him. Yet they remain far behind.

But the praise of errancy has its limits. Heidegger's mistrust of everything that does not belong to the thinking of being itself occasions mistrust. With the many references to errancy a certain escapism becomes possible in this thinking. Thus it can be objected here that in philosophy one should pay less attention, at any rate, to the dramatic narrative with its "grand" aberrations and more to the undramatic and tenacious fabric of the everyday and the all-too-everyday. Furthermore, we should not deny that the thought of the necessity of errancy can operate as an immunization of thinking. Sometimes there is a fine line between a deep insight into the character of thinking and a banal observation. Along with the precipitousness and the fall of the imposing thinker in the tragedy of being, there looms threateningly the danger of farce, indeed of buffoonery.

–

Philosophy is seldom comic. Philosophers, too. When Thales, contemplating the sky, fell into the well, the Thracian girl laughed. A typical accident. Heidegger can only note that this shows that philosophy is a thinking "which has no use" and "which serving-girls must laugh about."[83] It makes sense that philosophy has an ambivalent reputation for so-called common sense. Yet why shouldn't a philosopher who sees another philosopher stumble in theoretical loftiness laugh, too?

Comedy – it too is a narrative, a possibility for narration. Heidegger's time was not suited for being played out as comedy. One does the thinker an injustice if one reproaches him for having had no humor. One's laughter, too, can wither away. And if one's life is traversed by two World Wars and the Shoah, it is not one's place to laugh.

Yet, comedy is not exhausted in being amusing. While tragedy is great, insofar as it shows those who err, those who die, comedy is great insofar as it shows those who err, those who live. There is hardly a more profound depiction of erotic drama than Ingmar Bergman's *Smiles of a Summer Night* (*Sommarnattens leende*) from 1955. It is a comedy of sorts, but at the same time concerns the most sorrowful experiences. And there is a kind of serving-girl, who laughs a whole lot.

Yet Bergman's film means nothing within the field of Heideggerian thinking; it cannot mean anything within it. This is not to reproach either Heidegger or Bergman. Their experiences of the world are too distinct, their interests too distinct. We know how films appear that someone familiar with Heidegger shoots. Terrence Malick's *The Thin Red Line* from 1998 is an interpretation of *Being and Time*; a magnificent film that is only superficially a film about war.

There is nothing about comedy, about the comic, in Heidegger's published writings. That is an observation, not a critique. Narrative has no obligation to be total. For that reason the historiographic critics of Heidegger grasp at straws. They demand what the thinker explicitly refuses. Moreover, the comic perspective is missing in historiography, too.

The absence of comedies in his narrative is nevertheless noteworthy in one regard. When Sophocles died, Aristophanes was approximately 30 years old. Along with the great tragic poets, he belongs just as much to the Greeks beloved by Heidegger. They obviously not only tolerated but even enjoyed that Aristophanes caricatured the philosopher, namely Socrates, in the *Clouds* as an unscrupulous sophist. They even perhaps enjoyed that the uncanniest god, Dionysus, is absurdly parodied in the *Frogs*. It is immensely comical how he rows with Charon, whom he calls "potbelly," over the sea of the dead and croaks in competition with the frogs. Who were the Greeks, that they could laugh about their gods? What would Heidegger have said to the comic philosopher, to a comic performance of the "last god"?

–

Bertrand Russell has made the so-called liar's paradox well-known to us: "Epimenides the Cretan said that all Cretans were liars."[84] Ultimately this has nothing to do with a genuine paradox, for the result of the proposition is the falsehood of the statement, for which reason there must therefore still be a few Cretans who do not lie. We find the genuine liar's paradox in the statement: "I confess: I am lying right now." I cannot speak the truth and lie at the same time.

What we are saying with regard to Heidegger's references to errancy has nothing to do with the liar's paradox. The philosopher does not take errancy to be an aspect of consciousness, but rather to be a thinking, as it were, that can and must err even in its consciousness. The statement is never the indicator of such errancy, but rather the one erring rushes "objectively" to his doom. He simply does not know what is happening. He is as though blind.

Nevertheless, Heidegger's thoughts on errancy have a confusing consequence for the reading of his texts. If the author of a text presupposes that everything could be errancy, that indeed errancy necessarily belongs to the paths of thought, then an immunity comes to be formed against the denial of a thought as false or even as errant. The first can be overcome, as it is difficult in any case to demonstrate mistakes to a philosopher. The second is problematic, however, for when errancy becomes a necessity of thinking, it loses its character as deviation from the truth, as loss of the passable path.

Furthermore, one can no longer illustrate when thinking errs and when it does not. Certainly, there are Heidegger's own belated concessions, for instance, in regards to his engagement with National Socialism. Yet the texts themselves that testify to this engagement present themselves as free from error. And does the statement that all genuine philosophical thinking must err not lead to the possibility that even the concession of errancy can be a trace of errancy?

At no point did Heidegger signal that he was deceived in those anti-Semitic passages.[85] He was silent about this, as he chose to be silent in regards to the Shoah. Even if he had conceded that he had made a great error, even in the best case the only thing that would have followed from that would have been that a true philosopher must necessarily err in his ventures.

Heidegger's talk of errancy deprives the reader of the possibility to oppose his thinking without having to reject it altogether at the same time. This is one of Heidegger's measures for putting the readers of his texts under pressure. Like a seducer erotically dramatizing the world of the seduced and thereby turning the world upside down, the thinker continually sets before those thinking along with him the decision to give it everything they've got or else to give up. Many do not hold firm under this pressure and become either infinitely tractable admirers or haters. Only another kind of philosopher can, in his freedom, view Heidegger as a friend and at the same time refuse him unconditional allegiance.

–

If it is right that Heidegger's anti-Semitism belongs to the semantic field of the *Protocols of the Elders of Zion*,[86] then Heidegger's thinking moves here too in a narrative – in a narrative, by the way, the history of whose reception has not yet reached an end. It is a narrative in which thought an-archically goes astray. Resoluteness toward errancy – enter: "World Jewry."

For about a decade, anti-Semitism was the "uncanniest of guests"[87] in Heidegger's thinking. The question as to how this could happen ignores the appropriative event of errancy. It would be just as presumptuous to assert that the catastrophes of world history are testimonies of errancy as it would be to opine that the subjects of these catastrophes would have always known everything about what happened and their entanglement therein. Can, then, a single subject ever be responsible for an entire world war? For Heidegger, it was clear that thinking is exposed to the "abyss of freedom." It errs, and for errancy there is neither responsibility nor guilt.

At the end of his life, as it came time to decide the order in which his *Nachlass*, that doubtlessly most beloved corpus to him, would be published, it is very well possible that Heidegger regarded the *Schwarze Hefte* as a trace of errancy in the sense of his an-archic thinking. Freedom, the letting-be of things and human beings, demanded that the corpus be left untouched. Where there is no outside of errancy, errancy cannot be avoided. Without pangs of conscience, Heidegger decided in favor of an unchanged publication.

This decision can have a constructive side. "Perhaps," Heidegger says at one point, "even my *errors* still have a power to prod in an age that is overloaded with correctnesses which have long lacked the truth."[88] The traces of errancy are certainly prodding. They stir something up that cannot be integrated into the logical understanding of truth. Irrespective of the question as to whether Heidegger's judgment about modernity is right, to see the thinker fall appears to be a unique drama. Today, no thinker falls anymore.[89] By publishing this material, did he wish to confront us with this fact?

Of course, no one can answer this question. Perhaps he intended something else; perhaps something escaped him. Work on the *Nachlass* ultimately had to be brought to an end, simply because his powers dwindled. Yet the thinker would have fallen back behind his thinking if he had retouched the sketches. Loyalty to thinking is loyalty to errancy. The *Schwarze Hefte* are the authentic testimony to this loyalty.

The one who errs is without guilt. The thought that Heidegger could have somehow apologized for his thinking is weak. His silence [*Schweigen*] is here and there certainly also concealment [*Verschweigen*]. It is also correct that, after the destruction of the "Third Reich," he proceeded tactically, thought up strategies. Yet in the end his thinking remained true to itself in silence. When Heidegger admitted his error publicly, he made concessions.

The question is how we stand with respect to such a thinking, how we bear the fact that a philosopher with such lack of responsibility frustrates ideas and expectations of morality. Did Heidegger not see what was happening with the Jews? Did he not know of the obligation to support them philosophically? Is there perhaps no responsibility of the philosopher, of the author, of the artist, etc.? This question is a refusal of an-archic freedom. Whoever poses it complies with a normative morality. Today no one is exempted from helping; it is normalized. That it happens more often today than in Heidegger's time belongs to the lies that are also normalized.

The question concerning responsibility conflicts with a thinking that contests the validity of the question. To decide on this conflict marks *the limit*. Whoever holds responsibility to be an indispensable element of thinking and acting will find no confirmation in Heidegger's thought. Whoever attempts to inhabit Heidegger's thought must abandon the expectations of responsibility and guilt. This limit has become clear after the publication of the *Schwarze Hefte*.

–

The ordinary conception of philosophy presupposes a responsible philosopher, a subject related to itself. It appears that the philosopher in this regard is even a special kind of subject. Must not reflection illuminate a self that is all the more responsible the more it reflects? The philosopher – the conscience of the times.

Duty is inscribed, as it were, in the philoso-phizing soul. It reads in itself the appeal to express only what is justifiable. The philosopher is the universal human being, who cultivates the universe of the other; advocate for ruler and the oppressed, the rich and the poor. If no one else has a clue, he must know. For, he knows what is first and what is last. And his metaphysical sleeplessness drives him still further beyond.

Where the living human being is already rational as such the philosopher just becomes a reason-machine; he becomes a robot that com-putes human well-being. The philosopher must exorcize the human frailties of passion, injustice, bigotry and ignorance. To be sure, he loves, but he loves reason.

Admittedly, here too it is not immediately clear with which voice the philosopher speaks, if it is that of the universal human being, the voice of reason. To hear this voice, is this not an expro-priation that is fulfilled by the fact that what is heard is to be repeated? The philosopher as an interrogator of reason, a vanishing porousness in the logical production of the world.

For Heidegger that is an indication. No one is master of the house here. It is the "history of beyng" that "casts the dice."[90] It "allows for the appearance that human contrivance [*Menschen-mache*] determines how they fall." The subject ascribes to itself the production from which the rules of life emerge. There is nothing other than this subject – the integration of the world is perfected in it. Yet that is a misunderstanding, an ontological misunderstanding.

The roll [*Fall*] of the dice is determined by the "slant [*Gefälle*]" on which truth eventuates. "Only those who are ascending" know this inclining angle of truth. These are without doubt the thinkers. They expose themselves to the throw of truth, to the ac-cidental chance [*Zu-fall*] of an unavoidable determination completely without ground. But even the "ascending ones" do not become masters of truth. Indeed, philosophers are "players," and yet they are "only players who get played."[91] The "player who is played" – free and at the same time given over to fortune [*schicksalsergeben*].

Philosophers speak with a borrowed voice. What they say they never say in their own name. They are the echo, a response that is never to be held responsible. That is an ancient thought. Thinking thinks itself – a deep insight into the appropriative event of philosophizing. The philosopher is only wholly a philosopher when he undergoes the tragedy of the truth. He ascends in order to fall – not into the well but into the volcano.

–

Nothing provoked more anxiety in Heidegger than the possibility of "historylessness."[92] The "*poem of the world*"[93] is the play-space of his thinking. "Historylessness" is poem-lessness, is the loss of the narrative, of tragedy, of plot, also the loss of being able to set an example, in Nietzsche's sense, of the philosophical life. The "disenchantment of the world" (M. Weber) is totalized into an omnipresent normalization of thinking and acting. Moral responsibility takes the place of tragic action; the argument takes the place of tragic thinking.

Imre Kertész has spoken of the "Auschwitz-narrative," of Auschwitz as "an indispensable part of the European mythos."[94] At first sight, this way of speaking is legitimate. There can be no question that Auschwitz has become the source of a series of unforgettable narratives. Auschwitz has become "Auschwitz," a narrative, a mythos. Auschwitz is what cannot be narrated; "Auschwitz" is the narrative. "Europe" is also "Auschwitz."

To this extent, the Shoah belongs to the poem of the world; it is located beyond "historyless-ness." For this reason, Kertész, like Paul Celan's friend Peter Szondi,[95] controverts Adorno's thought that "To write poetry after Auschwitz is barbaric."[96] For Kertész "after Auschwitz one can only write poems about Auschwitz," a hyper-bolic turning to the mythical character of "Aus-chwitz." The echo of "Auschwitz" resounds everywhere in the "poem of the world."

But in that case the *Protocols of the Elders of Zion* and "Auschwitz" belong together. They belong to the grand narrative of errancy that Heidegger tells. Not that he would have actually spoken of the one or the other, not that he would have expressly taken them up into his distinctive narrative of the history of being. Yet where the world presents itself as a narratable history, Hei-degger's thinking remains, the *Protocols* remain, "Auschwitz" remains, possible. That Auschwitz was actual, remains a trauma.

Going astray, erring, the *Protocols* and "Aus-chwitz" belonging together? They do so in a manifold way that is not to be known. No doubt we distinguish harmful from useful myths. Yet is that a criterion? The plausibility of the narratives must doubtless be distinguished. But the phantasmata, the fictions, the lies, belong to history. They haunt us, disturb us, hound us into errancy. And to whom is that said in a world in which the virtual has for a long time undermined what is becoming ever less clearly real?

In the end, Heidegger's thinking appears once again in another light. Is not "Auschwitz" only possible in the poem of the world? Would not Heidegger, then, be the philosopher who, errant in the *Protocols*, saved "Auschwitz"? "Errancy-fugue" and "Death Fugue" would belong together.[97] The history of being is a history of errancy. It offers a place for all that is "immense" and "monstrous." It itself belongs to this "monstrousness."

—

The "encounter between Celan and Heidegger" was characterized as "a quasi-mythical episode of our epoch."[98] That the encounters between poets and thinkers can contain a mythic significance is a Heideggerian thought. Alain Badiou inscribes himself, together with it, into a dramatic narrative. Even for him history remains a narrative (hence, too, the epochal role of the "Cultural Revolution," etc.).

Badiou does not doubt that Celan could not ignore "the most complete silence about the Extermination" in Heidegger. Yet the significance of the encounter is extended. Celan wanted to learn from Heidegger what the task of philosophy was as the twentieth century was petering out. "Yet this philosopher referred to the poem, precisely in such a way as to make the poet feel more alone in his presence than ever before." Yet Celan "could" likewise "experience here what the philosophical fetishism of the poem ultimately produced," namely the failure of thinking in respect to its engagement with National Socialism.

"The most profound sense of his poetic work," however, "is to deliver us from this fetishism, to free the poem from its speculative parasites, to restore it to the fraternity of its time, where it will thereafter have to dwell side by side in thought with the matheme, love and political invention." Celan's painful relationship to Heidegger was certainly also influenced by a skepticism toward an idea that asserted the superiority of poetry over thinking. Yet the question is whether Heidegger was committed to this idea.

Heidegger's fidelity to poetry is not connected to his subordination of thinking to it. There are passages in his thinking that suggest such a hierarchy, yet there are also others that suggest the opposite. Heidegger thought that history eventuated as a poem of the world. He believed that he could recognize the trace or the origination of this poem in errancy. He thought that he had found the source of the poem.

Celan was able to see in Heidegger the philosopher someone who, on the basis of thinking, could give the most extensive meaning to the poem in history. In this gift the poet recognized himself – as painful as that was. Certainly, Celan wanted to learn how and why Heidegger could not break his silence. He sees how he "chokes on his errors [*Verfehlungen*]," how he "does not pretend he never did any wrong"; he sees someone "who does not conceal the guilt that clings to him."[99] And certainly, he would have unconditionally rejected an ethics of errancy and emphasized the responsibility of the poem. Yet beyond this he found in Heidegger the thinker who, in the impending poem-lessness, or the poem-lessness that had already occurred, caught sight not of the catastrophe but, what is perhaps worse, of the impossibility of catastrophe. Poem-less – loss of even the catastrophe.

–

We live in a world of the argument. Perhaps it stems from, and serves, technicity, a functional thinking that subordinates itself to technicity. Perhaps it stems from, and serves, the well-being of humanity. The argument – key to a world that renounces mythos. Its truth, rationality, does not bounce off the narrative. It annihilates it. Whatever claims to be a narrative or mythos is seen through. The truth of the argument also destroys the mythos that "Auschwitz" is a shape of rationality itself. It is borne by a sobriety that is committed to detail. Detail is the norm of the argument. It is the end of all "greatness."

To argue against the truth of the argument is a performative self-contradiction. All forces that attempt to do so must acknowledge their complicity, or they make themselves ridiculous. "To be against something" was never so difficult as it is today. This is already implicit in the fact that this "against" must bow to the conditions against which it wishes to proceed. To be outside the argument means to be outside the world.

Technicity is the "house of being."[100] If there were no narrative tone, we could confirm the sentence. Technicity has become too common-place for the histories of provenance and autoch-thony to still be taken seriously. It forms the center point of our dwelling, whence it has always already come. There is therefore also no longer any possibility to be "against technicity." Irrespective of the fact that it has never merely been the sum total of apparatuses, they have meanwhile formed a presence of absolute imma-nence. We dwell technically, i.e., within the medium. Our sobriety does not allow us to make any grand story [*Geschichte*] out of that. That corresponds to the argument. It regulates digres-sions. We gladly get caught up in networking, perhaps a little decadently, yet in the main with enlightenment and tolerance.

Whether or not there is a normative ethics in the truth of the argument is not important. The sobriety of detail does not allow itself to be beguiled into "greatness." If it organizes the small goals of life pragmatically, efficiently, and with infinite correctability, we can be certain of the "truth of democracy."[101] It needs no alpha and no omega. It is the bee of commonplace life, which tells itself stories of the most measured intimacy in order to share them with like-minded people. In public, there prevails a somewhat boring kind of communication that nevertheless has the great advantage of minimizing the dull frustration of the dissatisfied. Not at all a bad thing, that they don't say what they are thinking. No one loves the argument, yet that is no argument. It lacks any alternative.

There is an argument even for narrative. Film is this argument's best object. It thereby generates in the world a virtual sphere in which subjects can satisfy their narrative needs. There are arguments for considering film as a descendant of tragedy. It serves to purge [*Abbau*] the state of affect. The claim that there was no longer any narrative was therefore not sober, not detailed, enough. Viewed more closely, the world is full of narratives. Yet it is itself no longer one.

Poetry was always an appropriative event of intimacy. It had world-founding power only where the argument had not yet been normalized. The normalized argument knows, however, what it has on poetry. Thus there are more poets today than ever. The medium lets them get the attention that their work on language merits. Thus the poem, too, takes part in this world that lets anyone and everyone take part who wants to.

The drama of thinking has vanished in the world of the argument. It conforms to the sought-after applications in which it proves its usefulness. Even the question as to whether philosophy is still possible in this world founders on detail. The question itself begins to lose its contours, its significance.[102] What there is, what there isn't, who wishes to say? Nonsense, to want to escape arguments. Discourse functions. No catastrophe in sight.

Notes

1 *Irrnisfuge: Heideggers An-archie* (Berlin: Matthes & Seitz, 2014).

2 English translations include *Poems of Paul Celan*, rev. and expanded edn, trans. Michael Hamburger (New York: Persea Books, 2002), 31; and *Selected Poems and Prose of Paul Celan*, trans. John Felstiner (New York: W. W. Norton, 2001), 31.

3 *Hölderlin's Sophocles: Oedipus & Antigone*, trans. David Constantine (Highgreen: Bloodaxe Books, 2001), 81 [trans. mod.].

4 Martin Heidegger, *Nietzsche: Erster Band* (Pfullingen: Neske, 1961), 9; *Nietzsche: Volumes One and Two*, trans. David Farrell Krell (San Francisco: HarperCollins, 1991), vol. 1, p. xxxix.

5 Martin Heidegger, *Der Anfang der abendländischen Philosophie. Auslegung des Anaximander und Parmenides* (GA 35), ed. Peter Trawny (Frankfurt am Main: Klostermann, 2012). [A translation is forthcoming as *The Beginning of Western Philosophy: Interpretation of*

Anaximander and Parmenides, trans. Richard Rojcewicz (Bloomington: Indiana University Press, 2015). A list of other English translations of Heidegger's *Gesamtausgabe* (including other forthcoming translations) can be found in Thomas Sheehan, "Heidegger's *Gesamtausgabe* and Its English Translations," *Continental Philosophy Review* 47 (2014): 423–47.]

6 Martin Heidegger, *Frühe Schriften* [*Early Writings*] (GA 1), ed. Friedrich-Wilhelm von Herrmann (Frankfurt am Main: Klostermann, 1978), unnumbered second page.

7 *Federbälle, Teil I und Teil II, mit Briefen von Carl Jacob Burckhardt und Martin Heidegger in Faksimile* [*Shuttlecocks: Part I and Part II, with Letters from Carl Jacob Burckhardt and Martin Heidegger in Facsimile*] (Zurich: Verlag der Arche, 1980). [This passage is also in *Martin Heidegger im Gespräch*, ed. Richard Wisser (Freiburg: Karl Alber, 1970), 25; translated by B. Srinivasa Murthy as *Martin Heidegger in Conversation* (India: Arnold Heinemann, 1977), 14 (trans. mod.). As Heidegger explains at the beginning of his collection *Holzwege* (translated here as "timber tracks"): " 'Wood' is an old name for forest. In the wood there are paths, mostly overgrown, that come to an abrupt stop where the wood is untrodden. / They are called *Holzwege*. / Each goes its separate way, though within the same forest. It often appears as if one is identical to another. But it only appears so. / Woodcutters and forest keepers know these paths. They know what it means to be on a *Holzweg*." Cf. Heidegger, *Holzwege* (GA 5), ed. Friedrich-Wilhelm von Herrmann (Frankfurt am Main: Klostermann, 1977) (unpaginated); *Off the Beaten Track*, trans. and

ed. Julian Young and Kenneth Haynes (Cambridge: Cambridge University Press, 2002) (unpaginated).]

8 [The German *unsicher* means both "uncertain" and "insecure." Throughout, we have rendered it both ways depending on context.]

9 Martin Heidegger, *Zum Ereignis-Denken* [Towards Thinking the Appropriative Event] (GA 73.2), ed. Peter Trawny (Frankfurt am Main: Klostermann, 2013), 904.

10 Martin Heidegger, *Heraklit. 1. Der Anfang des abendländischen Denkens. 2. Logik. Heraklits Lehre vom Logos* [*Heraclitus. 1. The Inception of Western Thinking. 2. Logic. Heraclitus' Doctrine of Logos*] (GA 55), ed. Manfred S. Frings, 3rd edn (Frankfurt am Main: Klostermann, 1994), 123.

11 Martin Heidegger, *Gedachtes* [*Thoughts*] (GA 81), ed. Paola-Ludovika Coriando (Frankfurt am Main: Klostermann, 2007), 44.

12 Was Heidegger acquainted with Celan's "Todesfuge" ("Death Fugue"), which was published in 1952? They were both already in contact by then, yet there is to my knowledge no evidence that proves Heidegger's acquaintance with the poem. And yet – considered from Heidegger's vantage point – the "errancy-fugue" is (the) "Death Fugue." For me, Celan's poetry in regard to the Shoah is, by the way, required reading.

13 Heidegger, *Gedachtes* (GA 81), 316.

14 [That is, the objective genitive and the subjective genitive. For example, "the love of God" can mean both the love someone has for God and the love God has for someone.]

15 [This is a literal translation of the German title of Trawny's book, i.e., *Irrnisfuge: Heideggers An-archie*.]

16 Martin Heidegger, *Sein und Zeit. Erste Hälfte* (Halle an der Saale: Max Niemeyer, 1927), 1; *Being and Time*, trans. Joan Stambaugh, revised and with a Foreword by Dennis J. Schmidt (Albany: State University of New York Press, 2010), xxix.

17 "The narrative function is losing its functors, its great hero, its great dangers, its great voyages, its great goal." Jean-François Lyotard, *The Postmodern Condition: A Report on Knowledge*, trans. Geoff Bennington and Brian Massumi (Manchester: Manchester University Press, 1984), xxiv. Unlike Lyotard, we shall find the senselessness of the "narrative function" unproblematic.

18 Martin Heidegger, "Der Ursprung des Kunstwerkes," in *Holzwege* (GA 5), 41; "The Origin of the Work of Art," in *Off the Beaten Track*, 31.

19 Martin Heidegger, *Aus der Erfahrung des Denkens* [*From the Experience of Thinking*], 2nd edn (Pfullingen: Neske, 1965), 17; "The Thinker as Poet," in *Poetry, Language, Thought*, trans. Albert Hofstadter (New York: Harper-Collins, 1971 [2001 Perennial Classics edition]), 9.

20 Cf. Ulrich Greiner, "Darf groß irren, wer groß dichtet?" ["Must He Err Greatly Who Poetizes Greatly?"], in *Zeit Online* 2006, Issue 24: " 'He who thinks greatly must err greatly,' said the German philosopher Martin Heidegger, when they held his entanglement in National Socialism against him. This statement, instead of showing remorse, betrays overbearing arrogance."

21 [Literally, "non-essence." *Unwesen* generally means "nuisance" or, as in the phrase *sein Unwesen treiben*, "to make trouble."]

22 Martin Heidegger, *Überlegungen XII–XV. (Schwarze Hefte 1939–1941)* [*Considerations XII–XV. (Black*

Notebooks 1939–1941)] (GA 96), ed. Peter Trawny
(Frankfurt am Main: Klostermann, 2014), 171. Heidegger speaks, for example, still in the winter of 1955–6,
of the fact that "autochthony [*Bodenständigkeit*]" has
been the presupposition "of every great age of humanity." Martin Heidegger, *Der Satz vom Grund* (GA 10),
ed. Petra Jaeger (Frankfurt am Main: Klostermann,
1997), 47; *The Principle of Reason*, trans. Reginald Lilly
(Bloomington: Indiana University Press, 1991), 30
[trans. mod.].

23 Heidegger, *Überlegungen XII–XV* (GA 96), 230.

24 Ibid., 243. Cf. my book *Heidegger und der Mythos der
jüdischen Weltverschwörung*, 2nd edn (Frankfurt am
Main: Klostermann, 2014). [Trawny's book has been
translated by Andrew J. Mitchell as *Heidegger and the
Myth of a Jewish World Conspiracy* and is forthcoming
with the University of Chicago Press.]

25 Jürgen Kaube: "Die Endschlacht der planetarischen
Verbrecherbanden [The Final Battle of the Planetary
Gangs]," *Frankfurter Allgemeine*, March 13, 2014, No.
61, 10: "In the strict sense it is not a matter of philosophy, for there are neither arguments nor reflection."

26 Trawny, *Heidegger und der Mythos der jüdischen Weltverschwörung*, 11.

27 Wolfgang Benz provides the criterion for this judgment:
Was ist Antisemitismus? [*What is Anti-Semitism?*]
(Munich: C.H. Beck Verlag, 2005).

28 Friedrich Nietzsche, "Schopenhauer als Erzieher," in
Unzeitgemässe Betrachtungen (KSA 1), ed. Giorgio Colli
and Mazzino Montinari (Berlin: De Gruyter, 1980),
350f. "Schopenhauer as Educator," in *Untimely Medita-
tions*, trans. R. J. Hollingdale (Cambridge: Cambridge
University Press, 1983), 136f.

29 [Ibid.]

30 Martin Heidegger, *Überlegungen II–VI. (Schwarze Hefte 1931–1938)* [*Considerations II–VI. (Black Notebooks 1931–1938)*] (GA 94), ed. Peter Trawny (Frankfurt am Main: Klostermann, 2014), 31.

31 Ibid., 248.

32 Martin Heidegger, "Die gegenwärtige Lage und die künftige Aufgabe der deutschen Philosophie" ["The Present Situation and the Future Task of German Philosophy"], in *Reden und andere Zeugnisse eines Lebensweges* [Speeches and Other Testaments to a Life's Journey] (GA 16), ed. Hermann Heidegger (Frankfurt am Main: Klostermann, 2000), 333.

33 Nietzsche, "Schopenhauer als Erzieher," 417; "Schopenhauer as Educator," 187.

34 Ibid., 351/137.

35 [We have, unless otherwise indicated, rendered this term literally throughout, although generally it means "leeway" or "elbow room." It has a more positive sense than these in being a space or open realm in which things can happen or something can unfold.]

36 "Still a principle, but a principle of anarchy." Reiner Schürmann, *Le principe d'anarchie. Heidegger et la question de l'agir* (Bienne/Paris: Diaphanes, 2013), 15; *Heidegger on Being and Acting: From Principles to Anarchy* (Bloomington: Indiana University Press, 1987), 6. I share a similar interest with Schürmann. Yet, much has happened between 1982, the first appearance of his book, and 2014 – by which I do not mean only the publication of a great number of volumes of the Collected Works.

37 Martin Heidegger, *Überlegungen VII–XI. (Schwarze Hefte 1938–1939)* (GA 95) [*Considerations VII–XI.*

(Black Notebooks 1938–1939)], ed. Peter Trawny (Frankfurt am Main: Klostermann, 2014), 81.

38 Immanuel Kant, *Kritik der praktischen Vernunft*, ed. Hort D. Brandt and Heiner F. Klemme (Hamburg: Meiner, 2003), A 277; "Critique of Practical Reason," in Kant, *Practical Philosophy*, ed. and trans. Mary J. Gregor (Cambridge: Cambridge University Press, 1996), 264 [trans. mod.].

39 Martin Heidegger, *Parmenides* (GA 54), ed. Manfred S. Frings, 2nd edn (Frankfurt am Main: Klostermann, 1992), 119, 125; *Parmenides*, trans. André Schuwer and Richard Rojcewicz (Bloomington: Indiana University Press, 1992), 80, 84.

40 Heidegger, *Zum Ereignis-Denken* (GA 73.2), 1277.

41 Heidegger, *Überlegungen VII–XI* (GA 95), 417. Cf., also, Martin Heidegger, *Beiträge zur Philosophie (Vom Ereignis)* (GA 65), ed. Friedrich-Wilhelm von Herrmann (Frankfurt am Main: Klostermann, 1989), 374; *Contributions to Philosophy (Of the Event)*, trans. Richard Rojcewicz and Daniela Vallega-Neu (Bloomington: Indiana University Press, 2012), 296: "For the experiencing projection does not occur here as the representation of a general essence (γένος), but in an original-historical entrance into Da-sein's site of the moment. To what extent such an entrance in Greek tragedy?"

42 [The German is *Handlung*, which we have also translated as "action" and "deed."]

43 Martin Heidegger, "Brief über den 'Humanismus,'" in *Wegmarken* (GA 9), ed. Friedrich-Wilhelm von Herrmann, 2nd edn (Frankfurt am Main: Klostermann, 1996), 356; "Letter on 'Humanism,'" trans. Frank A.

Capuzzi, in *Pathmarks*, ed. William McNeill (Cambridge: Cambridge University Press, 1998), 271 [trans. mod.]. Cf. also Jean-Luc Nancy, *La pensée dérobée* (Paris: Galilée, 2001), 85–114.

44 Heidegger, "Brief über den 'Humanismus,'" 354; "Letter on 'Humanism,'" 269.

45 Martin Heidegger, "Vom Wesen der Wahrheit," in *Wegmarken* (GA 9), 188; "On the Essence of Truth," in *Pathmarks*, 144 [trans. mod.].

46 Ibid., 196f./150f.

47 [*Erkenntnis* in German means both knowledge or cognition and recognition (in the sense of tragic recognition, for example). Depending on context, we have rendered the term differently, though these various valences should be borne in mind.]

48 [Trans. mod.]

49 Ibid., 194/148.

50 Heidegger, *Beiträge zur Philosophie (Vom Ereignis)* (GA 65), 22; *Contributions to Philosophy (Of the Event)*, 20 [trans. mod.].

51 Ibid., 24/21 (my italics).

52 Cf. my text *Adyton. Heideggers esoterische Philosophie* [*Adyton: Heidegger's Esoteric Philosophy*] (Berlin: Matthes & Seitz, 2011). Alongside a philosophical seriousness that involves the question concerning another concept of "knowledge" than the scientific one, there is also a scientific-sociological side that has had a harmful effect in Heidegger studies. While there can be no doubt that, by "knowledge" as a relation to the "truth of beyng," Heidegger was thinking ultimately about philosophical thinking and living, "Heideggerians" have understood it as a call to unconditioned partisanship of Heidegger's

own thinking. For them it holds that Heidegger never errs. That is – as he himself emphasizes – a misunderstanding.

53 Heidegger, *Zum Ereignis-Denken* (GA 73.1), 584.

54 Right at the beginning of the Introduction to his *The Theory of Communicative Action*, Habermas writes: "The theory of argumentation thereby takes on a special significance; to it falls the task of reconstructing the formal-pragmatic presuppositions and conditions of an explicitly rational behavior." Jürgen Habermas, *Theorie des kommunikativen Handelns, Vol. 1: Handlungsrationalität und gesellschaftliche Rationalisierung* (Frankfurt am Main: Suhrkamp, 1981), 16; *The Theory of Communicative Action, Volume 1: Reason and the Rationalization of Society*, trans. Thomas McCarthy (Boston: Beacon Press, 1984), 2.

55 Heidegger, *Zum Ereignis-Denken* (GA 73.2), 1072.

56 Aristotle, *The Poetics*, trans. Stephen Halliwell, in *Aristotle: The Poetics. "Longinus": On the Sublime. Demetrius: On Style* (London: W. Heinemann, 1932), 1450a38.

57 *Sophocles*, Volume Two, ed. and trans. Hugh-Lloyd Jones (Cambridge, MA: Harvard University Press, 1994), ll. 1025ff.

58 Martin Heidegger, *Hölderlins Hymne "Der Ister"* (GA 53), ed. Walter Biemel (Frankfurt am Main: Klostermann, 1984), 108; *Hölderlin's Hymn "The Ister,"* trans. William McNeill and Julia Davis (Bloomington: Indiana University Press, 1996), 87 [trans. mod.].

59 Martin Heidegger, *Überlegungen XII–XV. (Schwarze Hefte 1939–1941)* (GA 96), ed. Peter Trawny (Frankfurt am Main: Klostermann, 2014), 202.

60 Jean-Luc Nancy, *La pensée dérobée* (Paris: Galilée, 2001), 19.

61 Heidegger, *Sein und Zeit*, 245; *Being and Time*, 236.

62 Heidegger, *Beiträge zur Philosophie* (GA 65), 118; *Contributions to Philosophy*, 93.

63 Heidegger, *Sein und Zeit*, 243; *Being and Time*, 234. Heidegger, *Beiträge zur Philosophie* (GA 65), 410; *Contributions to Philosophy*, 325. [The translators of the latter render *Reife* as "maturity."]

64 Aristotle, *The Poetics*, 1450b25.

65 Heidegger, *Überlegungen XII–XV* (GA 96), 274.

66 Heidegger, *Zum Ereignis-Denken* (GA 73.1), 844.

67 Heidegger, *Überlegungen XII–XV* (GA 96), 251; Heidegger, *Zum Ereignis-Denken* (GA 73.1), 845.

68 Heidegger, *Überlegungen XII–XV* (GA 96), 238.

69 [We are following Sean Kirkland's translation of *Medium* as "medium" in his translation of the two preliminary remarks of Trawny's book *Medium und Revolution* (Berlin: Matthes & Seitz, 2001). Cf. "Medium and Revolution," trans. Sean Kirkland, in *Being Shaken: Ontology and the Event*, ed. Michael Marder and Santiago Zabala (Basingstoke: Palgrave Macmillan, 2014), 85–91. This term comprises and entails more than what we typically mean by "media," though the latter should be kept in mind as well.]

70 Cf. my book *Ins Wasser geschrieben. Philosophische Versuche über die Intimität* [Written in Water: Philosophical Attempts Concerning Intimacy] (Berlin: Matthes & Seitz, 2013).

71 Hannah Arendt, *Between Past and Future: Eight Exercises in Political Thought* (New York: Penguin, 2006), 5.

72 Martin Heidegger, *Feldweg-Gespräche (1944/45)* (GA 77), ed. Ingrid Schüßler (Frankfurt am Main: Klostermann, 1995), 120; *Country Path Conversations*, trans. Bret W. Davis (Bloomington: Indiana University Press,

2010), 78. [Trawny is referring to Heidegger's first "Country Path Conversation," entitled "Ἀγχιβασίη: A Triadic Conversation on a Country Path between a Scientist, a Scholar, and a Guide."]

73 Friedrich Nietzsche, *Also Sprach Zarathustra. Ein Buch für Alle und Keinen* (KSA 4), ed. Giorgio Colli and Mazzino Montinari (Berlin: De Gruyter, 1980), 128; *Thus Spoke Zarathustra: A Book for All and None*, trans. Adrian Del Caro (Cambridge: Cambridge University Press, 2006), p. 77.

74 I am of course aware that §§54–60 of *Being and Time* are occupied with "conscience" and "guilt." They provide astounding insights. Yet irrespective of the fact that "guilt" and "conscience" here hardly have anything to do with a normative morality, Heidegger never took up the theme again. Something appears to have hindered him from such an otherwise customary reconsideration.

75 *Sophocles*, Volume One, trans. Hugh Lloyd-Jones (Cambridge, MA: Harvard University Press, 1994), ll. 924ff.

76 Ernst Tugendhat criticized precisely this in Heidegger's understanding of truth in his influential dissertation on the *Wahrheitsbegriff bei Husserl und Heidegger* [*The Concept of Truth in Husserl and Heidegger*], 2nd edn (Berlin: De Gruyter Verlag: 1970), 389 ff. It remained in a "precritical immediacy." Only the "affective cast of our conceptions and representations" would yield an indication of the true and the false. I would go further and claim that not even an "affective cast" can organize the difference between true and false.

77 Heidegger, *Hölderlins Hymne "Der Ister,"* 94; *Hölderlin's Hymn "The Ister,"* 77 [trans. mod.].

78 Heidegger, "Brief über den 'Humanismus,'" (GA 9), 359; "Letter on 'Humanism,'" 272.

79 Martin Heidegger, *Anmerkungen II* [Remarks II], 153. In *Anmerkungen I–V. (Schwarze Hefte 1944–1948)* [Remarks I–V (Black Notebooks 1944–1948)] (GA 97), ed. Peter Trawny (Frankfurt am Main: Klostermann, forthcoming 2015).

80 Hannah Arendt, *Eichmann in Jerusalem: A Report on the Banality of Evil* (New York: Penguin, 1994), 288.

81 Heidegger, *Überlegungen VII–XI* (GA 95), 227–8.

82 ["Der 'Irrende' müsse 'auch ertragen, daß ihm das Falsche und Verfehlte und Zwei- und Mehrdeutige,' worin er stehe, indem er es noch fördere, 'als das Eigentliche seines "Wollens" vorgerechnet und damit das ganze seines Denkens dann verworfen' werde."] Martin Heidegger, "Anmerkungen II," 106, in *Anmerkungen I–V* (GA 97).

83 Heidegger, *Zum Ereignis-Denken* (GA 73.1), 432.

84 Bertrand Russell, "Mathematical Logic as Based on the Theory of Types," *American Journal of Mathematics* 30 (1908): 222.

85 Perhaps with the exception of a poem for Hannah Arendt. Cf. Trawny, *Heidegger und der Mythos der jüdischen Weltverschwörung*, 105 ff.

86 I have postulated this thesis in my book, *Heidegger und der Mythos der jüdischen Weltverschwörung*. It has been criticized, because I could not prove that Heidegger had read it. I cannot concede the objection. The concept of "World Jewry" already belongs in itself within the context of the legend of a Jewish world conspiracy. As soon as one employs it one moves within a narrative that the *Protocols* develop. They are characterized by Wolfgang Benz as a "Text-Incunabulum"

with an "absolute reference-character" (Benz, *Was ist Antisemitismus?* 192). Heidegger accordingly goes astray in a narrative that he does not have to have studied. It is the errancy of his anti-Semitism.

87 Friedrich Nietzsche, *Nachgelassene Fragmente 1885–1889* (KSA 12), ed. Giorgio Colli and Mazzino Montinari (Berlin: De Gruyter, 1980), 125; *Writings from the Late Notebooks*, trans. Kate Sturge (Cambridge: Cambridge University Press, 2003), 83.

88 Heidegger, *Überlegungen II–VI* (GA 94), 404.

89 Could it be that Jürgen Habermas' corpus will be one of the first in which simply nothing at all prodding can be found anymore? Heidegger, Wittgenstein, Adorno, Sartre, Arendt, Derrida, Nancy, Badiou, even Gadamer, everywhere one stumbles upon dissonances. Normalization takes hold. The philosophy of the future – integration brought to completion.

90 Martin Heidegger, *Die Geschichte des Seyns. 1. Die Geschichte des Seyns. 2. Κοινόν. Aus der Geschichte des Seyns* [The History of Beyng. 1. The History of Beyng. 2. Κοινόν. From the History of Beyng] (GA 69), ed. Peter Trawny, 2nd edn (Frankfurt am Main: Klostermann, 2014), 213. [A translation by William McNeill and Jeffrey Powell is forthcoming as *The History of Beyng* with Indiana University Press (Bloomington).]

91 Heidegger, *Zum Ereignis-Denken* (GA 73.1), 612.

92 Heidegger, *Überlegungen XII–XV* (GA 96), 131.

93 Martin Heidegger, *Bremer und Freiburger Vorträge. 1. Einblick in das was ist. 2. Grundsätze des Denkens*, ed. Petra Jaeger, 2nd edn (Frankfurt am Main: Klostermann, 2005), 56; *Bremen and Freiburg Lectures: Insight into*

That Which Is and Basic Principles of Thinking, trans. Andrew Mitchell (Bloomington: Indiana University Press, 2013), 53.

94 Imre Kertész, *Eine Gedankenlänge Stille, während das Erschießungskommando neu lädt. Essays* (Reinbek bei Hamburg: Rowohlt, 1999), 52, 88, 85.

95 "After Auschwitz, no poem is possible, except on the basis of Auschwitz." Peter Szondi, "Durch die Enge geführt. Versuch über die Verständlichkeit des modernen Gedichts," in Szondi, *Celan-Studien*, ed. Jean Bollack with Henriette Beese et al. (Frankfurt am Main: Suhrkamp, 1972), 102f.; "Reading Engführung," in *Celan Studies*, trans. Susan Bernofsky with Harvey Mendelsohn (Stanford, CA: Stanford University Press, 2003), p. 74 [trans. mod.].

96 Theodor Adorno, "Kultur und Gesellschaft," in idem, *Kultur und Gesellschaft I. Prismen. Ohne Leitbild* (Frankfurt am Main: Suhrkamp, 2003), 30; "Cultural Criticism and Society," in: *Prisms*, trans. Samuel and Shierry Weber (Cambridge, MA: The MIT Press, 1997), 34.

97 I am of course by no means claiming that Heidegger's thinking and Celan's poetry simply belong together. That would ignore the painful problem that is found in this constellation and that the *Überlegungen* and *Anmerkungen* confirm. What I want to say is that Heidegger's thinking approaches poetry and its self-understanding. It sounds a little strange, yet it is clear that Heidegger attributed to poetry a greater significance than Habermas did. Habermas nevertheless has reasons for his decision.

98 Alain Badiou, *Manifesto for Philosophy. Followed by Two Essays: "The (Re)turn of philosophy itself" and "Definition*

of philosophy," trans. and ed. Norman Madarasz (Albany: State University of New York Press), 86–7.

99 *Herzzeit. Ingeborg Bachmann / Paul Celan. Der Brief-wechsel,* ed. Bertrand Badiou, Hans Höller, Andrea Stoll, and Barbara Wiedemann (Frankfurt am Main: Suhrkamp, 2008), 118; *Correspondence: Ingeborg Bach-mann and Paul Celan,* ed. Bertrand Badiou, Hans Höller, Andrea Stoll, and Barbara Wiedemann, trans. Wieland Hoban (London: Seagull Books, 2010), 181.

100 Heidegger, "Brief über den 'Humanismus,'" 313; "Letter on 'Humanism,'" 239. There one of course reads: "Language is the house of being."

101 Jean-Luc Nancy: *The Truth of Democracy,* trans. Pascale-Anne Brault and Michael Naas (New York: Fordham University Press, 2010).

102 The universal normalization in the unity of technicity, capital and the medium integrates everything, thus philosophy, too. There are approximately eight different types of integrated philosophy:

1. an enlightenment type of controlling, moral-socio-logical critique;
2. the technical-scientific type that is entirely bound to the functionality of technicity and science (ana-lytic philosophy, the philosophy of mind);
3. a type that reacts to the practical questions of appli-cation emerging from technicity (applied ethics, etc.);
4. a very timely type of affirmation of the commodity-character of philosophy made possible by and demanded in the unity of technicity-capital-medium, which does not shrink from pseudo-non-

conformist worldly wisdom (sometimes packaged as an "Asian art of living");

5. a type that is integrated as the seeming refusal of integration;

6. a type that seeks (in vain) to withdraw from the unity of technicity-capital-medium by an intensification of the philosophical stance;

7. a type of Christian rectification;

8. an academic type that indeed hardly stirs, as it were, in the face of widespread conformity, yet can still at least avoid the commodity-character of thinking (which of course represents a weakness in the perspective of the unity of technicity-capital-medium).